Dharma Bøards

Manifesto— Pt. 2

Justin Dalrymple-Kelly
Dharmaboards@gmail.com

(Intermission)

<u>Act V</u>

Chapter 37

"When I close my eyes all I see is the tunnel. I can't stop its acceleration. Just endless deeper black rings," Adam said, distant.

Adam and Maya walked the wooded late morning hillside. Adam grabbed a waxy leaf and broke it into bits without thinking as he walked along behind Maya, climbing or stepping over brush.

"What is that tunnel? I saw you there, in front of it that day." Maya asked.

I don't know. It's not good. For one thing it's where their armies come out," said Adam.

Maya could sense Adam's lingering trauma. She looked to her surroundings for the answer.

"Remember when we were lost in those woods? Before ever talking to a coyote?" she asked.

"Yeah. Good times," Adam said, half joking.

"We sat in that stump and things where looking pretty bleak. But then, there was a point." Maya said. "The sun must have been on the other side of the world, and then —an inflection point of light— really only a lighter dark, but it was something you sensed. That light was gonna come, and nothing was gonna stop it."

Maya looked back at Adam. Adam looked up at Maya, understanding as he stepped.

"We got you, Adam, the dark is over," she said with a face nobody was gonna shake.

Adam's face became a copy. The forest gave way to a nearby mountain peak. Adam and Maya took in the view of the river and meadows below, and the snow topped peaks in the distance.

"Zeddefungo came to me in the cave," said Adam looking ahead.

"What? Zeddefungo?" said Maya turning towards Adam in disbelief.

"He appeared to me on an image projected across his board," said Adam, turning to Maya.

"What did he say? Where was he?" Maya asked.

"He told me to dig down and hold on," Adam told her. "He told me you guys were coming. I don't know if I would have made it that night."

Maya looked out over the scene.

"I don't know where he was," Adam said. "There were others I could see, passing behind him. It was just green light, hard to tell."

"This is amazing," Maya said as she began down the trail. "Let's get back to camp. Maybe Ubuntu or Mom know where he was."

Adam followed with a little laugh.

"What?" Maya said, turning as she walked.

"Mom!" Adam said to Maya smiling. "I just can't believe it. I can't believe she's here."

Ubuntu and Dharma were washing berries and mushrooms they had gathered when they saw Maya and Adam approaching in the distance.

"You're looking bright, Adam," said Dharma.

"I *feel* brighter. I feel lighter," Adam said coming across the grass.

"Good, we'll need to continue North today, if you are up to it," Ubuntu said. "I believe you are ready."

"Yep, let's do it!" Adam answered.

"Wonderful," said Dharma. "We'll come to some towns later today. It's about time you get out of that musty old cloak."

"It's about time," Ubuntu smiled. "It's just not your style. Not to mention you are swimming in it."

"Must be a one-size-fits-all— thing," Adam laughed.

"Ah," Ubuntu laughed. "It's truly good to have you back Adam."

Maya was at her bowl of berries and wild mushrooms.

"Oh, Adam, tell them— who you saw," said Maya.

"Zeddefungo, on his old board, in green light," Adam said. "Is he alive?" Adam asked.

Ubuntu and Maya looked at each other.

"I don't know if 'alive' is the right word," said Dharma. "But somewhere, he is somewhere, it would seem, carrying on in some form, able to translate his being to you."

"I'm optimistic," Ubuntu said smiling. "I sense Zeddefungo's spirit. But Dharma is right. It is not how I sense you or Maya."

"We could use that trickster right now," said Dharma. "No matter, I expect he has a plan."

"Zeddefungo? A plan?" Ubuntu let out a big laugh.

Dharma could not help but laugh.

"Okay. I know. Maybe passing over does something to you." Dharma said.

Maya and Adam looked at each other, unable to see what was so funny.

"Alright, we better get moving if we want to make into town at a decent hour," Dharma said. "By that I mean you guys make it into town. I'm not really dressed for the occasion. Ubuntu, you might pass for— "

"No, I'm good," Ubuntu laughed. "Cities are not my thing."

Ubuntu, Dharma, Adam, and Maya packed up camp and got to riding. They passed out of the mountains and crossed into tan plains, green plains, tree lines, rock walls, farmland.

Chapter 38

They made camp in no-man's land, a ways outside of town in an old field near an island of trees, on a steep slope not fit for crops, or sheep, or anything. Just a few odd trees existed in its shape. A dirt road ran into town along a stone wall. Adam and Maya glided at an easy pace, keeping an eye out for cars or people.

They came into the town at sunset. —Brick streets, brick buildings, stucco buildings, alleyways. The street lamps were just turning on. It was a town of moderate size. People passed gaily in the streets, or busily, wearing long coats, leather coats, and no coats.

The roads curved through two- or three-story buildings— pubs, apartments, businesses. The road climbed hills, stopped at parks with fountains, winding trails, before going back downhill again. Trees with no leaves dotted the streets, blew in the wind and hit sticks of branches together as Adam and Maya passed underneath, holding their boards.

"I would have predicted more awkward staring," Adam said. "They don't seem too put-off by a boy in a cloak with a stone board. Where are we?"

"I don't know— Europe?" Maya said. "Anyways, let's find a shop before they're all closed."

Adam and Maya passed through the streets with swiveling heads looking for some kind, any kind of clothing store.

"I guess I did already see two guys in black cloaks so far," Maya said, looking around.

"They sure close their stores early in this town too," Adam said passing yet another "closed" sign in a window. "Don't they have a Wal-Mart?"

They passed down an alley where the sign above some door was still lit.

"Agh. It's just another pub," Maya said. "Well," she continued, and then turned towards the open alley, "how about dumpster clothes?"

"No way... I'm not wearing any nasty, thrown out, stranger's clothes," Adam said. "Especially not in another country."

"Well, we'll have to come back then. First thing in the morning," Maya said.

Adam took a few running steps, dropped his board and hovered up a loading ramp, ollied off of that into a wall ride, landing a 180, crashing onto a can and glass filled bag of trash.

"Adam!" Maya ordered, looking around.

"What?" Adam protested. "There's no one around."

Adam rode away and hopped up on a hand rail that dropped off, and landed a big 180 kick flip, coming down on a dumpster, another 180 off.

"Alright! Let's get out of here," Maya said. "You look like the King of the Goth's. Don't you have an underground Metal Concert to get to?" Maya said jokingly.

"I wish I did!" Adam said, taking off his hood, stuffing his board under his arm, when suddenly a little crash came from behind them.

A little glass bottle clinked and bounced in the alley. Adam and Maya froze and looked at each other. A couple stifled whispers and some shushing came from back in the alley.

Adam and Maya started walking briskly toward the alley exit. They were just about to break into a run when another louder crash came from behind one of the dumpsters, followed by some giggling.

In the darkness they could see a little kid roll into the moonlight of the alleyway.

"Jaccapo, you're cut off!" said a voice from the shadows.

"Come and make me!" said the child-like figure, charging back into the shadows, followed by more crashing sounds.

"Hey! Enough! They're gonna leave!" said another voice.

"Wait! Wait! Oh, great riders!" said a figure coming from the shadows followed by three more kid sized people.

Suddenly the figures popped off wall rides and grinds as they rapidly approached. Adam and Maya stood still, slightly confused.

"I've never seen a human who could ride," one of them said.

Promptly appeared the four little boarders, about as tall as Maya's shoulder. Adam and Maya were taken aback to see these figures were not children at all, but some kind of wooden humans. They were painted but the paint was fading. They had wooden rods for arms and legs connected by a pin at elbow and knee joints. They had a torso of round block with tapering accented shape, with a head of wooden block and a chin that actuated when they spoke.

"Hello, fellow riders," one of them spoke. "I am Tzara. We were out on a ride and realized your boards don't have wheels, yet they are quite animated, no?"

"Yes," Maya answered. "Who are you guys? Or, what are you guys?"

"We are—" Tzara began.

"We're puppets! Puppets that can ride! I'm Jaccapo," one said.

"I said, do not use the 'P' word Jaccapo!" said Tzara turning over his shoulder.

"Come and make me!" Jaccapo retorted, and the puppets where soon in another scrum.

"Excuse me," said Tzara gathering himself, brushing off his wooden figure. "We are simply— wooden beings. Our creator died at the end of his mortal life, many, many years ago, and left us wooden rider orphans."

"You poor things!" Maya said, reaching out a hand.

"Don't touch!" Tzara said slapping her hand away. "That was over 300 years ago. We have learned how to get by."

"My name is Ignatz," another one said. "How do you do?" he said extending his hand.

Adam shook his wooden hand.

"And I'm Anastasia," said another. "I make sure these buffoons don't kill each other. As well as put them back together when they bust themselves to pieces."

"Thanks, Anastasia," said Ignatz.

"So, what are you guys doing here anyways?" Tzara asked.

"We just came into town to get my brother new clothes," Maya answered.

"Oh, that's not how he usually dresses?" Tzara asked.

"No, it's not how I usually dress," Adam said. "But I'm much more interested in these shredding puppets now."

"No puppets," Tzara pointed. "But yes, let's see what we have in the way of clothes back at our theatre. It's just down the alley, and to the left, and to the right, and around the corner."

"We should really get back," Maya said.

"Come on. They have clothes," Adam argued.

"I thought you guys was just big puppets," said Ignatz.

Maya looked at the four wooden figures in front of her, in various levels of eccentric, fading, 1700's circus paint.

"Fine. You need a win after that stint in the cave," Maya said.

"Exactly!" said Adam. "How often do you get the chance to cruise with— wooden beings?" he said looking to the puppets.

They nodded.

"Alright," said Maya. "Take us to your theatre."

Chapter 39

The puppets rode, slashing and carving through the alleys. Tricking off any obstacle they could find. They were quite creative.

"These puppets have some style!" Adam said to Maya.

"Well they better have some clothes," said Maya.

They decelerated in front of a run down, old, old theatre. Like older than lights and stuff. It just had a wooden sign protruding in triangular fashion from the crumbling old brick. A sign that (barely) read 'Cabaret Vivo II' hung above the theatre. The windows were boarded up and spray painted.

"Low profile, yah know?" said Jaccapo.

Maya and Adam entered the theatre after the group of wooden persons. Through the doors there was a mezzanine. An old stone figure head of an elephant stood between two doorways, each with tattered maroon curtain for a door. On either side of these entrances were staircases leading up and leading down, a hallway on each side. The carpet was ancient and filled the room with a nice musty smell.

"Welcome to our own little Bohemia!" said Tzara leading the group through the curtains.

Passing through the curtains the group came out onto a balcony. Below was a grand old theatre and stage with seating all around. There were box seats protruding from the walls on either side. All was completely out of sorts. There were strings of light bulbs going every which way.

On stage were puppets playing cards and sitting bar at makeshift places. There were puppets in the seating watching movies on projectors eating popcorn. There were puppets playing instruments, jamming piano, guitar, twenty tambourines and African drums. But most of all there were puppets riding all manner of features in the theatre: rafters, balconies, backstage, half pipes. It was quite the sight to take in.

"We don't even eat really. We just like the popcorn in our mouth," said Tzara.

They came out on the ground level, walking as they looked around at all the commotion. Tzara took them to an area made of walls of sheets on three sides.

Tzara began throwing old clothes around from a chest. Dresses, puppet hats, sheets, blankets.

"Anything you want. It's yours!" said Tzara.

"There's nothing here but hats and dresses," said Adam as he sifted through the clothes.

"Right," said Tzara. "And that is... is that a, no?"

Adam stared.

"Jaccapo, Ignatz, clothes? Anybody?" Tzara asked them.

"We don't have need for many clothes," said Jaccapo.

"Right... Well," said Tzara.

"You don't have any clothes?" Maya asked astounded.

"Nope," said Tzara. "Looks like no clothes. Ah! But we have money. We have a pile of money, which we have no use for. It's yours!"

"Great! We'll just wait 'til morning and soon as a shop opens we'll be on our way," said Adam cheerily.

"What about Ubuntu and mom?" Maya asked taking him aside.

"They don't seem to worry much. They're all 'go with the flow' you know?" Adam said.

Maya looked around at all this, then looked at Adam's dopey grin.

"Alright, but you have to wear one of these old dresses 'til morning," Maya said. "I'm sick of looking at the black cloak."

"Great!" said Tzara. He smiled cheekily. "How about some sightseeing then?"

Adam took the black cloak off and picked an old 1940s white prairie dress with tiny polka dot pin drops and yellow flowers.

"Nice choice," said Anastasia.

She looked with concern at the stone board under Adam's arm.

"Although, the board is kind of clashing with the flowers," she said.

"This thing?" Adam said. "I hate it. I used to have a lightning fast board made of wood from the bark of giant sequoias or something."

"Hmm...," said Anastasia. "Well, we do have more than just hats and dresses. We are in no shortage of boards. Come on!" said Anastasia.

Adam followed Anastasia backstage where boards and old props laid scattered.

"Any one you want." Anastasia said. "They're good, too. Quality boards made by our maker, or emulated by Ignatz our master craftsman."

"Ignatz? Master craftsmen?" Adam asked in disbelief, looking over his shoulder.

"Yes, he has a way with woods," Anastasia answered.

Adam grabbed through the piles of boards until he found a beautiful Carmel colored natural wood with shiny glazing finish. On the board was a kooky trumpet and artistic lines of backdrop patterns.

"Cool!" Adam said looking at the board.

Adam and Anastasia rejoined the group.

"That's much better," said Maya. "It really brings out the flowers and goes with the pin dots."

"Thank you. I'm just going to take that sincerely," Adam answered.

"Follow me!" said Tzara.

They clambered up the stairs, as the puppets wooden feet clip clopped up. They continued up above the balconies into the darkness of the stairway.

"Who's ready for a night on the town?" Tzara said.

"I am," said Ignatz.

"Zip it, Ignatz!" Tzara snapped. "I'm sorry, Ignatz. You do like our little rides, don't you buddy?"

"Don't call me buddy for three days."

"But Ignatz. Buddy," Tzara said

"—I said three days!" Ignatz shouted.

"Ugghh," sighed Tzara heavily.

Ignatz shoved the handle and the old door swung open into midnight air. The puppets, followed by Maya, and Adam in his dress, stepped out onto the rooftops overlooking the city. Adam put his board down and tested it a little, apparently encouraged by its here handling.

"What if someone sees us?" said Maya.

"I don't know. I think they see us all the time," said Jaccapo shrugging. "I mean, we try to stay hidden, so a kid doesn't see us out his bedroom window, spurring nightmares—"

"Wonder!" Tzara interrupted "Spurring wonder."

"Magic." Anastasia added.

"Let's ride!" said Ignatz, dropping in, gapping roof to rooftops.

Into the night they rode, bouncing from roof top to rooftop, spinning, tapping, grinding air conditioners, wall-riding taller buildings. They rode far and wide, from easy gaps to technical areas.

"This is amazing!" said Maya.

"See!" said Adam.

Maya laughed at the sight of his floral dress flowing in the moonlight.

"And your dress is to die for!" She said, cracking up.

Adam feigned anger, but the truth was that the two of them were enjoying themselves. Something they hadn't done in a while.

Adam and Maya caught up to the puppets who were hanging their feet off the ledge of the tallest building in town.

"Beautiful, isn't it?" said Tzara, sincerely.

The six of them looked out over grids of amber light stretching into the night. It was a clear azure-blue night except for a few clouds that huddled around the yellow half-moon. The stars twinkled. The brick buildings sat. People and cars still breathed life into the streets late into the night.

"I'm glad we decided to stay around, Adam," said Maya leaning on him. "In the morning we can set out, refreshed. And dressed according to our genders."

"Lame," said Adam.

Chapter 40

Maya awoke in the theatre seats in a nest of blankets.

"Adam. Adam!" She shook him. "We're late!"

"Late for what?" Adam moaned, muffled in a blanket.

"Come on!" urged Maya.

Adam stirred to his feet. He grabbed his board and put his cloak back on. They stepped over sleeping puppets to the area where Tzara and the gang were sleeping on the stage. Anastasia rose and woke the others. The group exchanged goodbyes.

"Good luck in your war," said Ignatz. "We hope you win."

"Thank you, Ignatz," said Maya. "It was a pleasure meeting you."

"Thanks for the board, man!" Ignatz blushed. "This thing is a diamond in the rough! You've got some skill."

"And here is the piles of money," said Tzara. "How much does clothing cost?"

He pushed about 800€ across the table.

"This should do it!" Adam said grabbing a couple bills, then a couple more.

"Good bye friends," said Anastasia. "If you are ever in the area, don't forget to stop by."

"Or just change your plans and come here and stop by!" said Jaccapo, unable to stay reserved.

"We've never met human riders." said Anastasia, excusing Jaccapo.

And with that they left the theatre, exiting into early morning light.

"Okay pick a store," said Maya. "We gotta go!"

"Okay, okay," said Adam. "It'll take two seconds, relax."

They entered the nearest clothing store. Adam promptly grabbed a pair of brown pants and a tee shirt with a pocket, and bought it quickly at the counter.

"Now, let us continue saving the world!" Adam said, clearly happy over his new clothes and his new board.

"I really feel like myself again," he said.

"I was getting kind of used to the idea of the dress," Maya jested.

Just then a moving truck screeched to a halt mounting the curb at Maya's feet. Out came two metallic, shades of bronze machines in armor. Hissing and spouting steam, they mounted their clanky, loose-leaf metal boards, pursuing the young riders menacingly.

"What the heck are those?" Maya shouted.

"I have no idea!" Adam shouted back.

The machines rattled through the alleyways. Each emitting a cloud of brown exhaust and closing in.

Adam and Maya reached a dead end within the brick maze.

"Up! Up!" Maya screamed.

But it was too late. Adam and Maya turned to fight, board on board, but the machine on the left, with old glass amber lights for eyes, produced a bronze cannon. Whirling and clunking, it fired off two wire nets. Adam and Maya were stunned and collected.

Maya's eyes went dim. Her eyelids fell shut. She and Adam lay on the wet cement of morning watching metal feet approach.

When they opened their eyes, they were being taken from the back of the moving truck and led by the robot men into a large, abandoned building. It was some kind of factory, with rows of broken, dusty windows. Inside, there were scattered lines of old rollers and tracks, and what was left of manufacturing equipment, with films of dust stuck to grease.

Maya looked at Adam drearily as the robots chauffeured them through a door and down. Down a flight of stairs, then down another, to some kind of sub-basement level. They entered what appeared to be a massive, broad, long boiler room. Pipes and furnaces lined the room as far as the eye could see. It was even larger than the factory floor, two floors above. It seemed to have its own horizon, to which Maya and Adam moved ever closer.

Other mechanical robots populated the furnaces and boilers, hard at work, with deranged, ancient mechanical smiles. They were such crude things by design. Tapered cylinders of brass, bronze armor. They had concentric pucks protruding from their shoulders, knees, and elbows. Their heads had old, telescoping-work around for circles.

The two robotic men dragged Adam and Maya down and down the aisle of the underground industrial metropolis. It smelled of phosphate and nickel-plated overheatings. The room was filled with brown, cast iron lines and bronze machinery pipes agreeing with the aesthetic of the mechanatronic beings themselves.

Finally, they came to some commander-and-chief sitting on a garrulous bronze throne of congruent, meaningless designs. He stood.

"I am Mazzatron, head of the mechanatronics," he said, waving his arm without meaning, bending slightly forward at the waist.

"What do you want with us, Multiple Irons?" asked Maya. "We have a previous engagement."

"You may be irreconcilably off schedule once we are done with you," Mazzatron said.

"And since you are already quite late, come, let me show you something."

Adam rolled his eyes. The robot lead them quite uncoordinatedly back through mazes of monotonous, animatronic work stations.

"You see, we provide a large chunk of what you see above with power of all kinds," the robot leader said.

"You burn coal? You're a power plant?" Adam asked indignantly.

"Not quite. I mean yes, but so much more!" said the machine.

He walked along as the subterranean metropolis opened up into a deeper, vaster expanse of mining, animatronic robots.

"We provide the highly sought after, highly exclusive— 'dark current!" said Mazzatron

"Never heard of it," said Maya.

"As you shouldn't," Mazzatron went on, "but I will educate you on the matter,"

"Mom's gonna kill us," Maya muttered to Adam.

"Dark current is a multidimensional form of power with applications far beyond those of basic electricity," said Mazzatron glancing at Maya and Adam. "How do you think we machines move freely, and what's more, live and think freely?"

"Artificial intelligence?" asked Adam.

"What?" said Mazzatron.

Adam looked at Mazzatron's assistant.

"I wouldn't use the term 'freely' for any of this," said Maya.

"Okay, that's enough!" said Mazzatron.

He led them to a large, iron cast chamber, with giant iron hinges and a small window.

"You are an especially fortunate catch," Mazzatron said. "In our energy farming sector, we catch and crush tens of puppets a day, endowed with the ancient power of the board."

"They didn't mention this," said Maya.

"Well they're not very bright!" Mazzatron said. "That's why they're our best customers, or should I say crop!"

He climbed the few grated steps to the front of the chamber.

"Now, it's very simple," Mazzatron said. "We shovel you into the large chamber— one at a time, two at a time, it doesn't matter. Then, we proceed to squeeze the life out of you, which our dark current transmogrifying device takes and turns into tanks of dark current for sale to the powers that be." said Mazzatron.

"Simple," Adam shrugged.

"—You're first!" said Mazzatron, pointing at Adam.

"No! Take me! Take us both!" said Maya, looking to Adam with a deep sense of bond.

"I love you, sister," Adam said, closing his eyes and hanging his head. "I'm glad we met mom."

"Nobody's mom is dying today!!" cried Jaccapo, flying in out of now where.

Soon swaths of puppets swarmed the underground city. They buzzed around busting the thin-walled brass machines left and right. With great speed they swooped and crashed through rows of robots.

"Do I have to deal with these blasted puppets myself?" cried Mazzatron. He produced a board from his back that transformed and extended, speeding away with a cloud of exhaust.

Tzara swooped in and kicking Mazzatron, sending his flimsy head spinning on his shoulders.

"We're not puppets, you dumb steam punk!" said Tzara.

Anastasia landed an aerial assault on the robot, holding Maya and Adam and their boards.

"Here you go!" she said, handing them their boards.

"Let's flatten these tin foil fools!" yelled Tzara.

The flock of puppets continued shooting westward and leftward across the room racking up casualties, sending limb plates flying.

Mazzatron rolled over. Pulling himself up, he pressed a large button beside a railing. Suddenly on the other side of the room a set of doors like jaws retracted open.

"You can beat up the workers all you want, but sooner or later you'll have to face the elite!" said Mazzatron.

Rows of soldiers poured out from the housing. The puppets rallied, joined by Maya and Adam, and met the combat robots mid-air in a shard-shattering, splintering crash, sending wood and metal everywhere.

These new steambots definitely had thicker shells. The puppets were being depleted.

"These guys are tough!" said Tzara. "At this point we usually retreat and eat popcorn!"

Maya looked around at the carnage. Then she noticed something.

"Yes!" she said. "Go! Get everyone out of here!"

Tzara pulled a bell out of a compartment in his torso. The puppets disengaged and sped away laughing. The robots followed close behind.

"Maya!" Adam shouted. "What are you doing? We had them!"

"Adam! Follow me!" yelled Maya, as she took off quickly.

She sped to the far side of the room and the wall overhanging an area of certain stations.

"Robots build more robots!" Maya said. "I'm sick of these animatronic maniacs!"

Adam was slightly aghast. He looked at the fleeing puppets nearing the exit.

"Now help me tip these pots!" Maya shouted.

She started pushing with her flat board sideways, powering through and tipping over the pot. Molten orange magnesium iron started spilling forth. Adam immediately sped to the other wall and started tipping pots.

Mazzatron descended upon them whirring and smoking.

"Do not touch!" he said, as he knocked Maya into the wall.

Adam came to her aid but in his mechanical rage, Mazzatron shoved him using his momentum, throwing him into the wall. Maya and Adam lie on the ground beside each other, physically injured, molten metal drawing nearer.

"I do not like the loss you have imbued upon my operation." said Mazzatron, growing sinister with anger.

Suddenly one puppet, two puppet, three puppet, four! Back and forth they strike! Anastasia, Tzara, Jaccapo, Ignatz coming to the rescue again, leaving Mazzatron bent and broken, sparking and twitching, trying to get up.

"And *I* don't like how many of my friends you turned into phone bills," said Anastasia.

Adam and Maya got up. Mazzatron was slowly beginning to be consumed with molten lava.

"The Dark Boards cannot be stopped," said Mazzatron eroding, "my operation is but a silver level donor to the well-oiled machine deeply entwined with our world."

"What do you know?" said Tzara. "You're just a puppet."

As Mazzatron was devoured by the glowing molten, his old amber headlight eyes powered down for the last time.

"We're not done here," Maya said mounting her board. "Tip the pots. All of them."

Adam and the group tipped the pots of the molten mixtures. The rest of the wooden beings made it safely out the exits. The remaining robot army turned on Maya. She tipped one more pot.

"Okay! Let's get out of here!" said Maya. "Adam! Pull these plugs!"

Adam looked around, searching for some kind of plugs. She started pulling massive cables from the ceiling, dislodging and disconnecting the chords. Adam did the same on the other side.

"Now go! Go! It's gonna blow!" Maya shouted, corralling Adam towards the exit.

They reached the exit just in time. Maya made sure everyone was out. She looked back once more at the metropolis. The cables of dark current came down emitting black-white sparks, white-blue bolts, purple flashes, crashing down into the molten lava rivers metal chemicals running. The reaction was beyond catastrophic.

"Let's go!" Adam shouted, looking through the door.

The six of them blasted up the stairs and out the broken windows of the upper factory, as it exploded into a cloud of black and orange and purple billowing smoke.

"Well," said Anastasia, floating on her board. "We won't be hearing from them again."

"You forgot to mention the animatronic army that hunts puppets like animals and juices them for power," Adam said, looking at the smoke."

"I forgot," Tzara said. "Yes, I try not to dwell on it."

Adam and Maya looked at Tzara.

"He— they— were our younger— *evil* cousins," Tzara said. "One hundred years our junior, they were made when metals and industrial revolutions were all the rage. We avoided any recognition—"

"—Low profile," Jaccapo interjected.

"They were employed, manipulated, by— I don't know, shadowy guys— in hoods. I don't pay attention," said Tzara. "We fly, they catch us, we eat popcorn, life goes on..."

"It's over now," said Anastasia, looking at the smoking building. "Let's go home,"

Chapter 41

At the theatre Maya and Adam sad goodbye once more.

"Why don't you come with us?" said Adam.

"I had no idea you were so skilled in combat," said Maya "We could use you guys up there."

"You mean it?" Tzara said, excited.

"But what about the others…" Anastasia started.

"They'll be fine here," Tzara said. "They won't even know we're gone."

"Well," said Anastasia, "I have always wanted to visit the north."

"Then it's settled," Tzara said. "I'm packed! You're packed!" he said, and looked towards the other three. "We have no stuff. We're good. Let's go!"

So, the puppets set out in broad daylight with the humans. When the people saw them in the street they were taken aback at first, but then they cheered and notified others of the amazing magic puppet show display.

"How are they floating?" they would ask. "Bravo! Bravo!" they cheered.

Over the hill they came, Adam and Maya in the early afternoon sun with new clothes, new boards, and new friends. Ubuntu and Dharma noticed them in the distance.

"You should have gone with them," said Dharma to Ubuntu, seeing the four new members.

Maya and the others approached the camp.

"Sorry, we ran into some— complications," Maya said, looking at the puppets who were smiling in the sun.

Ignatz bowed to Dharma and Ubuntu.

"I see," said Dharma, confused but nonetheless warm and inviting.

She was collecting bowls of raspberries and apples.

"I'm sorry," Dharma said. "We weren't expecting company, but please, let me collect a few more bowls."

"Oh, that's okay, miss," said Tzara, politely "We don't have much of an appetite. Actually we don't eat. But we do benefit from good company and good conversation."

He stepped forward humbly and extended a wooden hand.

"I am Tzara," he said. "It's nice to meet you."

"It's very nice to meet you, Tzara," she smiled. "I am Dharma."

The rest of the wooden beings introduced themselves to Ubuntu and Dharma. The four wooden beings and the four human beings gathered in the small dell outside of town. Adam and Maya explained the events leading up to their late arrival this morning.

"Valiant warriors indeed," said Ubuntu. "Thank you for your brave efforts. Without you, who knows what we would have done," she said looking at Adam and Maya.

"It is very good to hear of another victory in our favor. The Dark Boards lurk in all corners of the world," said Dharma.

"We figured they should come with us if they wanted," said Maya.

"Absolutely," said Dharma. "Even one could tip the scales."

Ubuntu was collecting the woven bowls and returning the camp to its natural state for their departure.

"There is no time to lose now," said Dharma. "Come. Old Tjikko is a two-day's journey."

And with that the eight beings glided north between the hills.

Chapter 42

The metallic army lined the cave from wall to wall. Shoulder to shoulder in organized legions, sectioned squadrons. They were standing, waiting, charging from the source. Their ironclad expressions were poised with all the power that the spoils of Adam's heart and the dark arts had to offer. Black smoke birds, by the hundreds, nested on high stone cliffs. They sparked and squeaked with dark electricity.

The storm continued churning at the tunnel mouth, far in the dark corner of the cave, grinding soldiers out in rows.

Radu rolled out an old papyrus map on the stone table in the high pantheon.

"We will make our way through Russia and approach Old Tjikko from the northeast," said Radu. "No need to draw attention at the moment. And an army of this stature would be sure to draw attention at the slightest sighting."

"Radu," said Arthur. "We are running out of room to store them."

"Good," Radu said. "Good. You can start to fill the village."

"It is nearly full," answered Arthur.

"Well fill the tunnels! We are close to launch!" said Radu.

"How many more are needed?" asked Arthur.

Radu stepped around the table to stand behind the hood of Arthur.

"Arthur" he said. "I don't know what this position of power is doing to your pride. But I have seven more men if you continue asking questions like this. I assume I could cycle through them if they all cannot follow— simple— orders— for more than one sitting!"

He leaned forward into Arthur's view.

"Would you like to join Marcus?" asked Radu.

Arthur was silent.

"Now you're quiet?" Radu screamed.

"No, my Lord. Continue," answered Arthur.

"I will continue, Arthur. Do you want to know why?" Radu asked. "I will continue conjuring soldiers until we have to lay them in piles, extending all the way to the ceiling! This contest is not an optional success. This victory is not a lofty wish. This is the undeniable fate of our empire! This is the destiny of our order!"

Radu returned to the head of the table.

"I will not allow the world to continue one second longer in weak and aimless triviality!" he slammed booming fists on the table in two clouds of dust. "The day we win, the day we conquer the pitiful Four Boardsmen, our existence begins its progress toward its full potential! "

Below, in the holding cells, Marcus sat back against the wall, flicking gravel. He raised his hood hearing Radu's screaming from above.

Soon Molek approached. He held a loaf of bread and a bowl of water.

"How kind of you," said Marcus.

"I would starve you if it wouldn't get me punished," said Molek.

"It's kind of nice down here," said Marcus. "Peace and quiet. No dealing with Radu's mania. A little dark, but where is it not dark in this cave?"

Molek pushed the bread and water through the grate.

"Anyways, when are we mobilizing?" Marcus asked. "I can't stay in here forever."

"Shortly," said Molek. "Lord Radu is wringing this spell dry, assuring no chance of our defeat. The soldiers line the walls of our village and begin to fill the tunnels."

"Lovely," said Marcus.

"I thought you were bent on avenging your father," said Molek. "Where has your zeal gone?"

"Things have changed," said Marcus. "It will take ages to even return to Radu's favor. That is if we even win. The best-case scenario is that he dies in our victory."

"You are not in much favor anywhere," said Molek.

Marcus dismissed him with a shooing gesture of his hand.

"You do know that I could take you, seven on one," Marcus said.

"I'll let you out right now and stomp you myself," said Molek, indignantly.

"A scuffle of that kind would not behoove me now," Marcus scoffed. "Probably just get us both killed."

"He needs us," Molek said.

"He doesn't even need himself right now!" said Marcus. "He just needs a rabbit for the troops to chase until they reach Tjikko."

Marcus stood and paced once down the cell.

"We will keep the Boardsmen busy while the metallic army does their thing," said Molek.

Marcus laughed out loud and said, "Is that the plan? Lord, if so, we're probably gonna lose."

"Do you want me to inform Radu of these sentiments?" asked Molek.

"I would prefer you didn't," said Marcus.

Marcus continued pacing, raising bread to his mouth, in the dim light of the prison corridors.

"You know, I'm not like you guys, Molek," said Marcus. "You, Arthur, Dracul, Moshe, etcetera. I'm not from the cave— creatures, whatever you things are. I'm like Radu." "We came from— elsewhere. Radu came down here to prove something, and he dragged me with him. My father— why am I telling you this? Who cares— you don't even care. My father was there for the schism of boards, when the Boardsmen rebelled against innovation, against efficient technological advancement, and harnessing the true power of the boards. Can you imagine?"

Molek stood stiff.

"Why am I in a cave?" asked Molek.

"Good question," said Marcus.

"I don't believe you," said Molek.

"Good. Follow that inclination," said Marcus.

He returned from the grated cell door to sit beside the bench along the wall and pulled his hood down further.

"Wake me when it's time to go," said Marcus.

Chapter 43

Dharma and Ubuntu lead the rest of the crew north through the countryside. The trees grew more green and plentiful, and countryside turned to forested land. Plains took on texture, wrinkling into hills and crags. A deeper green was fed by overcast skies and mist-cloaked vistas.

"I'm actually made from African mahogany," said Jaccapo, knocking with his knuckles up his torso to his head.

"An intelligent choice by your creator," Ubuntu said, gliding along the grass. "You will need all the robustness you can get."

"I'm made of clay," said Ignatz "The rest of us— all clay."

"What? Nobody is made of clay, you trout. I'm walnut."

"We all are made of clay." Ubuntu said. "Your friend has wisdom hidden in his–"

"Incorrectness..." interjected Tzara. "Hidden in his incorrectness?"

"Precisely," Ubuntu answered.

Tzara threw up his arms. Ignatz smiled, slightly shrugging his head in his shoulders

"Ubuntu is right," said Dharma "There are many orbits intersecting, patterns clicking."

This sent Tzara reeling. He turned away aghast, veering. Dharma smiled at Ubuntu.

"What the heck?" said Tzara. "What kind of circus did we join?"

"I apologize for my..." Anastasia paused and glanced. "Uh, brother, there were a lot of knots in the stock of wood he's made from. Very rude wood."

"Not a problem," Dharma said "Everybody serves their purpose."

"He's quite entertaining," Ubuntu said with a shrugging smile.

It was getting late. The overcast sky had broken, and pockets of navy, iridescent, violet sky, the last of the day poked through, dotted with stars appearing one by one.

"Here looks like a good place to camp tonight," said Dharma. "Let us gather firewood."

"AH!" Tzara cringed. "We don't say firewood. Too many good friends gone that way."

"Sorry," Dharma said. "Let's start a campfire."

"Okay," Tzara nodded.

The team gathered around the fire. A good time was had by all. They shared many a hearty laugh, deep in the secluded wooded forest, high atop a wooded hill, a sheer cliff of loose grey rock to one side, overlooking the starry night above the wooded valley.

"Thank you for the call to adventure, my friends." Anastasia said to Maya and Adam. "We don't get out of the city much. Actually never, to be exact."

"Glad you came," said Adam.

"Tomorrow," said Ubuntu "we are in need of a small group to return to the Tree of Life, to gather the troops, and return to Tjikko where we will be waiting for you."

"Ah, Africa," said Jaccapo. "My homeland. It would be an honor. I accept the mission."

"Our deepest gratitude, Jaccapo," Ubuntu bowed.

"I will accompany Jaccapo on this mission," said Tzara.

"Wonderful!" Ubuntu said.

"I can't," said Ignatz.

"Then it's settled!" Tzara clapped.

"Fine." Anastasia said, folding her arms.

"You'll set out first thing in the morning," said Ubuntu. "We need those warriors to Tjikko as soon as possible."

"Why wait 'til morning?" asked Tzara popping up. "We are accustomed to riding at night."

"A beautiful sentiment, but let us get some rest." Ubuntu said.

"We don't rest," said Tzara spritely "We don't sleep. We don't eat. We don't pee!"

Adam laughed. Even Maya giggled. Dharma smiled.

"Tzara and Jaccapo— night riders again!" Tzara said punching air punches. "Just one thing, how do we get to your— uh, place."

"Ah, yes. Hand me your boards," Ubuntu said.

Tzara and Jaccapo handed over their stained, glazed boards.

"I made those," Ignatz input.

"Thank you Ignatz!" shouted Tzara. Then calmly, "Sincerely, thank you, my brother."

Ubuntu took the boards.

"I'll embed the location of the Tree of Life within these two boards," Ubuntu said.

She sat and focused her attention on the boards. She closed her eyes. The boards began to levitate and glow. A path to the Tree of Life was burned into the boards.

"Oh, a roadmap?" Jaccapo said. "Okay. Nice."

"A bit more than a road map," Ubuntu said. "But yes, follow the path and you will find yourself at the Tree of Life. Tell them Ubuntu sent you, and they are to prepare for battle at Tjikko— with the swiftness! And, now..."

Ubuntu concentrated once more, burning yet another path into the boards, reaching upwards.

"This one is the path to Tjikko," Ubuntu said.

"You can count on us," Tzara nodded, then looked at Jaccapo.

"I know," Ubuntu nodded.

"Well!" Tzara said. Jaccapo and Tzara having boards in hand again. "What are we standing here for?"

"Good luck Tzara. Good luck Jaccapo," Adam said.

"See you at Tjikko," said Maya.

"May the Father of Boards protect your journey," said Dharma.

"Why? What's on it?" Tzara said.

"Probably nothing. I just say that," said Dharma.

Tzara bowed and they were off. Into the night they flew. And just like that, they were gone.

"I must admit. Those are some fast puppets," said Adam.

"They'll be back in no time," Maya said.

"Jaccapo and Tzara? Alone on a mission? If they make it there without ripping each other's dove joints out," said Anastasia.

"They will bond," said Ignatz. "It will be good."

Chapter 44

Maya roused herself slowly from her sleep. She sat up. Her blanket slid down and wrinkled in her lap. Adam laid there, mouth open, deep asleep. For it was early. The sun was cresting in the distance, creeping up on the horizon. The golden aura diffused into the hazy dew. All green surfaces glossy with moisture reflected shiny tinsel on the wooded hills. The low sun cast shadows in the subtle mist.

Maya rose and looked for Dharma and the others. She came to the edge of the cliff, at the end of the camp. Ubuntu, Anastasia, and Ignatz were below next to the stream, filling botas for the trek. Maya came down around the cliff side.

"Hey guys," she said "Have you seen my mom?"

"I believe she is just beyond that slope, tucked back in a hollow, you can't miss her," Ubuntu answered.

Maya crossed over the hill and found Dharma walking slowly down the ravine with board beneath her arm.

"Hey mom, what you doing?" Maya asked.

"Oh, just allowing the landscape to weave its way, with me in alignment, before we embark. It's a ritual I do," Dharma said.

"Right," said Maya. "Don't you worry? Aren't we late?"

"No, and yes," said Dharma. "Late for one way, here for another. My Maya, we have years of realigning coming. I love the feeling.

"It definitely would have been different with you here," Maya said.

"All the same," Dharma said. "Here, there, eventually..."

Maya rolled her eyes aside. Dharma knew it.

"I promise Maya, let it go, trust your heart. It won't confuse you," Dharma said.

Maya brought her face to Dharma. They walked.

"I'm trying. The war is not easy to stop fearing," said Maya.

"You may fear it," Dharma said dismissing lightly. "Fear it, but believe. Even fear is invited into the warmness of the house. I hold its hand, so it is not alone."

"Oh, mom. Where have you been?" Maya waned.

Dharma looked at Maya.

"Don't answer that," Maya laughed.

They walked along so slow.

"I was looking for you to ask if you would teach me the ways you showed Ubuntu. The energies. I could use them for the fight. Then I will believe— easy!" Maya said.

"Believe anyway," Dharma said. "Even if your leg is broken. Even if you're at the end." Dharma said. "—But —I will teach you. Sure. Let's get to this meadow."

They came into a clearing. A few birds took flight. A few deer stopped chewing and looked up.

"We won't hurt you." Dharma said.

Dharma sat on a floating board and gestured with her hand in front of her. Maya sat, face to face, several feet apart.

"I'll warn you this is— different," Dharma said. "You must know thy board on a deeper, wider level. You must realize it's not a thing that came to you, but is a thing that has returned."

They closed their eyes.

"The riders are a spirit, given a companion, given a soul— long before being came into form. Know your board like this. Soul from your being, one with your spirit, being from a dimension of treasures and talismans, energies," Dharma said. "Your companion, your guide, loaded with hidden abilities."

Dharma glowed with vapors rising. The deer stepped away into the forest.

"It draws from you and energy itself," said Dharma.

Maya opened her eyes. Dharma began to hum with energy. It swelled until—

"Direct it!" Dharma called.

The vapors beamed into the sky in brilliant white and yellow, streaks of faint orange and purple. The blast blew their hair back briefly, then quelled to a close.

"That is the essence of the power, how you strike with it will come, too," said Dharma. "First, we will summon this."

Maya closed her eyes and tried to tap into the place her mother took her moments prior. She felt her board as ancient soul creature and true part of her being. This she understood. She couldn't fully see the form of treasure, the realm from which in part the creature had its being. She could see it stirring in the distance. In the fringes.

"I see it," Maya said.

"Follow the light," Dharma said.

"It's faint," Maya said.

"See it," said Dharma. "Focus. Bring forth the light."

Maya began to vaporize energy about her. Softly these things hummed. Dharma's eyes brightened. Maya's brow furrowed and her aura trembled growing.

"Direct it! You have it!" Dharma coached.

Maya beamed a sapling light, releasing waving thread of purple energy into the sky. She lost form, a-gasp, and threw a leg up, losing balance. But out of her tilted board popped a little ball of energy, like a feisty bubble twirling, spiraling over Dharma's shoulder deep into the forest.

"Well," said Dharma.

Maya remained in shock.

"That was highly unpredictable," Dharma said.

Maya looked at her with wonder.

"No rider has ever even come close to summoning something in the early stages, let alone the very first attempt," Dharma said. "And now, you, albeit by accident, have shot a little vicious bubble out and nearly trimmed my ear off!"

"Sorry, it was an accident," apologized Maya.

"No, please, it was amazing!" said Dharma. "You should be proud of yourself. My lovely powerful daughter!"

Maya smiled then she hung her head a little.

"Well, it won't do me any good at Old Tjikko," Maya said

Dharma came to Maya putting an arm around her shoulder, giving her a hug.

"That will do you good in *all* things," said Dharma. "Trust me."

Maya smiled reluctantly.

"It was kinda cute I guess," Maya shrugged.

"Let's go with that," said Dharma. "Come. It's time we set out. Let's collect the others and be on our way."

Chapter 45

Radu swooped down through a row of soldiers with wild brazen fury, almost foaming at the mouth. He sped down long lines of the metal giants, flickering as he passed them.

"Now this is an army!" he yelled, with arms raised wide and trembling.

With a quick spin, he slashed his board, catching one of the soldiers in the face with a swift kick. The soldier, with cold un-phased stare, raised his hand to his chin and straightened his slightly crooked head on his neck.

"Hahaaa!" Radu shrieked wildly. He flew up to the skies and looked down on his army. "Children of the Dark Boards!" he screamed. "Prepare yourselves. Tomorrow we ride for glory!"

The soldiers jammed their heavy metal boards down in unison with two cave shaking booms.

"Remove this disease of weakness!" Radu said. "Children of the Dark— Boards! Stomp out the final flame of hope! Choke the last light from the earth!"

The soldiers jammed their boards once more, chipping into the cave floor with three deafening thuds.

Below, Marcus looked up as crumbling dust fell from the ceiling of the holding cell.

"Your dinner, good sir," said Molek, pushing through a tin plate with bread, and a tin bowl with water. "Tomorrow, we embark for Tjikko."

"I know," said Marcus, taking a bite from the loaf of bread. I can hear the old bat yelping from in here. He's gonna give himself a stroke. Wouldn't that be something."

Marcus took a drink from the bowl of water.

"Couldn't you have let me out before this fine dining then?" Marcus joked.

Molek was silent for some time.

"Molek?" asked Marcus, prodding.

"It is unclear if Radu has remembered to remove you from the cell," said Molek, looking up with some deviance.

"Well, could you mention something to him!" said Marcus, coming to the cell gate.

"It would be unwise to— distract him at the moment," Molek said.

Marcus breathed deeply.

"Good. Good. Yes. What will you have me in here then, rot?" he asked.

"There's a good start to a tunnel under that bench there." Molek answered, stepping closer to the gate. "Not all is lost."

"Fine. Great," Marcus said. "Well, good luck in battle I hope you—" Marcus struck with lightning swiftness,"—die honorless you slimy cave shrew!" And with hold of Molek's cloak, he slammed him repeatedly into the iron grate, until he fell unconscious to the dirt.

"I'll take these," said Marcus, removing the keys from his cloak. "Is it unclear *now* if I will be removed from the cell?" he said unfastening the door and stepping over the heap of Molek.

Marcus dragged Molek into the cell and locked it.

"I am tempted to stay to see Radu's reaction to all this, but alas—" Marcus turned.

Marcus grabbed a torch from the wall and scattered down the hallway. Down the tunnels he turned, having to remember how to navigate his way back here. He came to a large door in the high wall of the hallway.

"Aha!" he said.

He came into the big stone room with dirt and sand for the floor.

"Klatos, pack your things you're coming with me," said Marcus. "Just kidding, I know you don't have things. Now, come on. Before someone finds out what I just did to Molek."

Marcus stood with the torch, partially illuminating the dark of the room.

"Klatos?" Marcus said.

Just then a creature of a beast came roaring out of the shadows on a chain.

"Dark Mother!" said Marcus. "You scared me. Now keep quiet. Listen— to— me."

Klatos breathed very close to his face.

"I'm getting out of here, I greatly want you to come with me," said Marcus. "I— need you."

Klatos changed form slowly to the beast of a man, harry and snarling in the dark.

"Radu needs me, needs you, the Dark Boards needs us!" Klatos said, unintelligently.

"Radu... doesn't need you Klatos," said Marcus.

"I am valued," Klatos said.

"You are old news," Marcus said.

Klatos threatened, entered beast mode.

"But, not to me," said Marcus. "I fear Radu will leave you here to rot. Like he would have left me had I not been so cunning and wise. But you—"

Klatos jerked his head towards Marcus.

"Remember when I drew you out of the dark mouth?" Marcus asked quickly with his hands up. "When you were just a prisoner sentenced, most likely to death, with a small chance of experimental success?"

Klatos returned his head to reverie.

"Who pulled you out of that experiment?" Marcus asked.

"Marcus did," Klatos said softly.

"We go way back," Marcus said. "Now, let's get out of here. I know a place."

Back in the main cave.

"Lord Radu," said Dracul.

"Do not speak to me right now, Dracul," said Radu, intensely examining a scroll spread on altar.

"My Lord, you'll want to see this," said Dracul.

Radu followed Dracul down into the catacombs to find Molek lying in the cell where Marcus had been.

"What— are you doing?" asked Radu, with extreme tension.

Molek sat up dazed.

"Don't even answer. This is NOT THE TIME for playing games!" said Radu. "Search the cave for Marcus."

Just then Argon, one of the black hoods, entered the jail cells.

"My Lord— Klatos' cage— he's gone," said Argon.

Molek's head fell heavy under the stress of the situation. Radu turned his gaze on him.

"Marcus, Molek, what difference does it make," Radu said. "Enjoy your stay."

"Radu, my lord, no!" Molek beseeched. "You know my loyalty and devotion are unwavering. I beg you to allow me see the dawn of the age of the Dark Boards."

Radu took two slow steps forward.

"I won't make the same mistake.. of sending someone to feed you," Radu said.

"Oh, the horror, my lord, I will rot!" cried Molek.

"That's not completely true," said Radu, lightly. "I think there is a tunnel started for you under yonder bench."

"Noooooo!" cried Molek.

"Batten the hatches!" said Radu to Dracul. "I don't want to hear him crying all night. I must have the most fruitful of rests tonight."

Chapter 46

Dharma and the riders glide across the Baltic Sea in the solitude of the evening. The sun hangs low. The clouds transition from blue and white to orange and purple. The first stars of night begin to appear in the upper regions of the sky, where the sun has left the tapestry a silky early navy.

Forested stony islands dot the Baltic coast. The riders pass into the country, the endless hardwood forest, with age old agreements of space between the trees, age-old proper shade cover growing little or no brush beneath. Open forest. Stony hills and valleys. A little stream, a river valley.

"Welcome to Lapland," Dharma said. "This time tomorrow we'll be in Tjikko country."

Adam and Maya took in the landscape, seemingly invigorated by the forests.

"It looks like— home," Maya said looking warmly around.

"Let's make camp just ahead," Dharma suggested. "We can get a fire started right by the river's edge."

And so they did. Dharma and Ubuntu made the beds. Adam and Maya took care of the fire. Ignatz and Anastasia took care of filling the water bottles for the morning. Night fell and the riders sat encircled round the fire. Logs were sliced by Ubuntu's tested strength of new moves.

"Just want to see what this thing can do," Ubuntu said.

Ignatz stared wide eyed at Ubuntu chopping wood.

"Hey, maybe— let's see if it can cut a rock— or something," Ignatz quivered.

The riders passed around bowls of foraged mushrooms and berries. Dharma made a bowl of rice. The river flowed behind them riding over rocks, providing like white noise but life in all its chaos possibilities of water hitting rocks, and splashing hitting other water sounded like a line, until you listen closely to the chaos line across the prism boarder, speaking all the things the river knows, which is not just "go".

Adam was taking in the scene: the warmness of the crackling fire; the green gold trees; the fertile peat-moss dirt; and the silent river. The warm smiling faces of his friends and family on this wild adventure. They laughed and leaned on each other. Anastasia and Ignatz make a mockery of Mazzatron making Maya cry laughing.

"This is a dream come true," Adam said, looking at Maya and his mom, "being able to sit here with the two of you. All of you. Let's not go to war. Let's ride back to dad, and just surf the world for secret spots."

Dharma gave a compassionate little tilt of her head.

"That is just what I want to do Adam," she said. "But there will be no world to ride if the Dark Boards get to Tjikko."

Adam sighed and stared down at his feet. Dharma reached over a comforting hand on his shoulder.

"Only a chore, sweet Adam. Take the trash out before you go and play." She smiled reaching for his downcast eyes with hers.

Adam closed his eyes and smiled. "Okay, might as well go back to sitting with you in this dream then."

"The three of us, under the stars, in the flesh," said Dharma.

Adam's eyes gazed into the fire.

"I used to have these dreams, you know, but, I had to piece you together, from your pictures, from everyone's stories about you. But in my dreams, when I came to hug you, there was a blockage. There was some, signal, impeding me from hugging you. It must be 'cuz I..., well I could remember you from a picture; and some way be close to how you would be, how you would act— from stories— nice, and smiling warmly is good enough for me. But who can convey how it feels to be in your arms? To embrace someone. No one can," said Adam.

Dharma gave him a great big hug. "Oh Adam," she said.

Maya joined in.

Ubuntu put another log on the fire, smiling.

Anastasia and Ignatz hugged each other and started crying and sobbing.

"Sorry," said Anastasia sobbing. "Puppets are sensitive creatures."

"Alright, there there..." Ubuntu said, comforting the little ones.

An owl hooted in the night. The river ran schussing. The fire crackled red-orange deep, and sending smoke up to the stars.

"Oh!" said Maya, "you know how we're humans, but somehow we can ride the boards?"

"Um, yes," Adam said looking at Maya, glancing to the side awkwardly.

"Well..." Maya started.

She concentrated, closed her eyes and assumed a super peaceful state with eyebrows pulled up subtly. Suddenly she was a cat. A big, young, furry snow leopard perched sitting on her log.

"We might not be so human," Maya finished.

Adam spit out his rice. He looked at Dharma and Ubuntu then back at Maya.

"Yeah!" Maya said, sitting there. "Come on, mom. Show Adam the way."

"You're— you're a snow leopard??" asked Adam.

"So are you! Show him, Mom. Mom's a snow leopard too." Maya said behind her paw.

Dharma smiled.

"Yes, let us invoke your inner animal, little Adam," Dharma said.

Maya stood on her hind legs growling and clawing. Adam's eyes were wide open and bright.

"It's easy," Maya said "—well, kind of."

"Close your eyes Adam," said Dharma smiling. "Visualize your inner animal in space. Call to that faculty. Assign an object to that inner animal in your thoughts, and invoke that object. Bring it forth to being."

"Lure out the timid animal!" Maya half growled excitedly.

Adam looked uneasy and said, "I lured out a timid animal once in the backyard, it did not end well."

Ubuntu laughed.

"See it Adam. It has been inside you all along," said Dharma.

Adam closed his eyes.

"All you have to do," said Dharma "is to allow your human form to move aside, to release the wild side."

Adam concentrated digging deep, deep within his soul into his spirit. He felt a certain sensation.

"Something is happening," Adam said.

"Focus," Dharma said, low.

Adam's face let go. Suddenly the fire was the only crackling sound. The transformation was complete.

"What!?" said Maya, flabbergasted after awkward silence.

"What?" said Adam, wondering, opening his eyes.

"Wow." Ubuntu said.

Adam looked down at furry paws with claws.

"I did not see that coming," Ubuntu said.

"Is it bad? Is my arm coming out of my leg?" Adam panicked.

"Indeed, that is— interesting," Dharma said, staring in wonder.

"Somebody, tell me!" Adam said. "Puppet, tell me."

"My name is Ignatz," Ignatz said.

Maya crawled down from her post and lurked in front of Adam, with high leopard shoulder blades as she walked.

"You're— a coyote," Maya said.

Dharma looked at Ubuntu.

"I am?" Adam said excited "Cool."

And he began to yip and howl at the moon. The sound aroused the howls of a distant pack of wolves.

"Oops, maybe don't do that," said Adam.

He pounced around and pawed at Maya. They fought a little bit, back and forth, wrestling and biting each other's ears. Adam whimpered.

"Sorry," said Maya. "I don't know my animal strength."

Adam put his paws in front of his face.

"Awesome. I'm a coyote!" he sat.

Maya sat.

"Now how do I get back?" Adam asked.

"What is my animal?" said Ignatz stepping forward.

"Um, I don't think—" Dharma started.

"You just close your eyes and wish you were a llama or something?" Ignatz asked.

Suddenly he popped out of sight.

"Ignatz!" Anastasia shouted.

Ubuntu and Dharma exchanged looks.

He popped back into sight.

"Yeah?" Ignatz answered.

Ubuntu looked at Dharma, eyebrows slightly raised; mouth a little open, like she had something to say.

"Ignatz, you— you disappeared," Anastasia said in disbelief.

"Hmm, what kind of animal is that?" Ignatz asked.

Maya put her paw on her snout uncoordinatedly burying her eye.

The night went on. The fire died down. Anastasia demonstrated the ability of invisibility as well. They wished they knew this all along so they could get their popcorn in the daylight, and ride rooftops without giving children nightmares, or starting old wife's tales. Though they kind of liked that too. Maybe both were okay.

Chapter 47

"We're lost." Tzara said, hacking through the dense, humid under growth.

The puppets in the jungle, at the crack of dawn, did not know which way was up.

"Lost?" Jaccapo questioned him incredulously. "We have a map burned into the board. What do you mean, lost?"

The bugs of the night were bringing their symphony to a lull, passing the birds of the first shift arriving to pick up the slack. They cawed and blended their singing with the smaller monkey species.

"I mean I can't make my way in this dang, disorienting jungle, where everywhere I look is just the leaves of bushes in my face!" Tzara said, upset. "If I was just a foot taller..."

Just then he bumped into the back of a massive gorilla. He accidentally whacked the wood-like lower back muscles of the big black beast.

The silver back swiveled around quickly with its nostrils flared, searching, searching, overhead of lesser Jaccapo and Tzara. They had stumbled into the nesting place of Kuyu and his troop of silver backs.

Tzara trembled till his joints got loose and clicky-clacky.

"S-s-s sir?" Tzara stuttered.

Kuyu jumped back five feet.

"What in the jungle's mother is that?" Kuyu asked rhetorically.

"S-sir, um, we, have, happened to," Tzara started.

"Why... is this branch... speaking?" Kuyu spoke over; looking around to his troop to be sure they saw this too.

"We are lost, my good, kind sir," Tzara said.

"Incredibly lost, talking branch," Kuyu said. "You are from the sky then, yes?"

"What? No, we are from the Czech Republic," Tzara corrected Kuyu.

"Yes, another planet," said Kuyu.

"Um.. no," Tzara said.

"Animated talking branches?" Kuyu asked.

"No! No! We are wooden— beings!" Tzara corrected him.

"Sticks?" Kuyu asked.

"Puppets!" Tzara shouted. "We are called puppets!"

"Okay. Puppets!" The big gorilla said. "I have heard of those. I am Kuyu, head of the leading tribe of silver backs in the Congo jungle," said Kuyu proudly.

"Awesome. I am Tzara."

"I am Jaccapo."

"Oh my monkey god!" Kuyu flinched again. "There are two of you! I didn't see you their little man."

"Maybe you can help us," Tzara offered. "We're looking for the Tree of Life."

Kuyu became very inwardly defensive. He expunged hot breath from his nostrils in the cold of the jungle morning, and rose with inflated chest, towering above the puppets.

"Leave. Before I break you twigs in half," he said.

"We can't, sir," Jaccapo said, somehow somewhat stern.

Tzara looked at Jaccapo.

"Uh, that's right. Failure is not an option," Tzara said. "We need Ubuntu's army and we need them now. Are you on the side of good? Or are you on the side of Dark Boards?"

"Did you say Ubuntu's army?" the gorilla asked, deflating slightly.

"You know her?" Tzara deflated also. "Oh, thank goodness. Yes, the jungle goddess, Ubuntu herself has sent us on this all-important mission, to rally the troops! The troops of the Tree of Life."

"Why would she send—" Kuyu started.

"Never you mind that," Tzara said. "Now, can you get us back on course, my giant bareback friend?"

"How— all-important is it?" asked Kuyu.

"Your home could become a parking lot," said Tzara.

"That doesn't sound good," said Kuyu. "Hop on, little man. —Janco! Take the other wooden man."

"Do you guys need... food?" Kuyu said, looking at Janco "...Fertilizer?"

"No!" Tzara said. "We don't eat! Now take us to the Tree of Life!"

And off the quartet went, bulging through the jungle branches. Swinging, smashing, breathing deeply, panting. They went roaring, screaming, spooking flocks of birds, taking flight into the jungle morning.

In the Tree of Life, the people calmly eat their morning breakfast. They sit and meditate, relaxing on the rugs and hammocks, basking in the morning sun.

Nicu slightly lifted his head, alert in his hammock with a bowl of crickets slightly tipping over.

"Did you hear something?" Nicu asked.

"No," said Jatta. "I mean, hear what? I'm hearing a lot of things."

A distant cracking and crashing grows, closer, closer, crescendoing in a crash of two big black silver back gorillas, with a puppet each, aboard their backs. They came busting through the tree line, landing on the soccer field.

Nicu, Jatta and the elders descended the stairs immediately, meeting them in the field.

"A delivery." Kuyu announced.

"A message from the great Ubuntu!" beginning Tzara.

Elders looking face to face.

"Your presence is requested; I mean, as soon as possible. What I'm trying to say is—" Jaccapo said, exhausted. "Everybody, get your warrior-behinds up yonder Tjikko's way!"

"Whoa, slow down, slow down," said Jatta's dad. "Ubuntu sent you?"

"Yes, yes. Ubuntu. Hello, I am Tzara. Sorry, I'm so exhausted," said Tzara.

"I am Jaccapo," Jaccapo said. "Yes. Ubuntu sent us. We rode through the night."

"Tzara, Jaccapo, it is an honor to meet you, "said Kazzo. "I am Kazzo. Let us get you in the tree. You've had a long night. Maybe something to eat?"

"Sure," Tzara said. "Why not? Let's eat."

He passed out on jungle ground. The elders gathered round the great deck, surrounded by every warrior the Tree of Life had to offer, radiating outward, extending across all bridges and decks the Tree of Life had to offer in the morning sun.

Jaccapo and Tzara lay on the couches of the great deck with several men and women fanning them. Jatta and Nicu looked on in awe and preparation.

"There hasn't been such a battle since the schism of the boards." Kazzo said drastically.

"It's gonna be a big one." Tzara said, drinking water through a reed straw— trickling, and dribbling down his wooden bones.

"We will prepare to leave at once!" said Kazzo staring down and out. "I knew this day would come. I didn't know it'd come so soon."

"It's here, my friend," said Tzara. "We will need all the men and women we can get. If the gorillas could fly, I would take them too."

"Our boards extend," Jatta suggested.

"I like this kid," said Tzara.

The warriors gathered their boards and their belongings. They said their goodbyes to wives and children. They prayed to the Great Spirit this would not be the last time they held each other in their arms.

"Is Maya with Ubuntu, and Adam?" Jatta asked to Tzara.

"Yes, Maya," Tzara answered. "I love Maya. Adam's there too."

Jatta smiled.

"Kazzo," Tzara called. "How many warriors does this Tjikko have?"

"Tjikko? His elven army is unrivaled," said Kazzo. "He will double our forces at the very least. They have guarded Old Tjikko from the dawn of time."

"Double..." said Tzara. "I see."

He walked to the railing in the diffused late afternoon sun.

"You see," said Tzara, "the Dark Boards stole our little boy Adam's heart juice— soul force— and put a spell together hitherto unprecedented and impossible without the wonder twins here."

"I barely follow," Kazzo said.

"I'm just saying there are bound to be— numerous Dark Boards." Tzara looked around. "...I have an idea." He looked to Jaccapo. "Is the Czech Republic— on the way to Sweden?"

Kazzo looked at Jaccapo and back to Tzara.

"Well, it's not *out* of the way." said Kazzo.

Chapter 48

The team in Sweden set out north, for Tjikko. Dharma lead the riders up country through low-amplitude, long-wavelength land, shrouded in emerald forests. The river they followed came into higher country where the water went low, and the valley walls rose broad in wide berth. The riders trimmed the tree tops, followed the slow snake of the valley.

The sun was slowly leaking over the west rim of the valley. Dharma veered off the river, up the slope of the valley, and gradually the riders crested a peak. The river went right and the riders paused at the summit, looking north. The land stretched before them seeming never to meet the horizon. The colors of the trees and hills were defined and had simply slipped into the sky.

"Is this the end of the world?" Adam asked.

"Not quite." Dharma answered. "First, Tjikko."

The riders continued, crawled the climbing latitude. North, north across a vast golden-green sea of flat planes, scattered pine trees, blue-grey rocks tied to the blue-gray overcast sky. This colossal bowl like cradle crossed into the great unknown. All is ambiguous here.

They came to the end of the great bowl and ascended into dense forested shadowy pines. Slowly they crept through the woods, gliding and looking over their shoulders.

"I know it's near here somewhere," Dharma said. "It's been sometime since I've paid a visit to brother Tjikko."

"*What's* near here somewhere?" Adam asked, apprehensively.

It was getting very dark within this densely covered pine bough forest, firs looming left and right.

"The fortress of the elves," Dharma whispered. "It's a grand, stone castle. You can't miss it. Though it is a bit tucked back, in one of these ravines."

The riders searched the forest slowly.

"Dharma." Ubuntu said, with sudden piercing gravity.

As Ubuntu slowly approached a glen in the hills, Dharma came up slowly to her side. Their faces rang with horror, furrowed confusion. Ubuntu looked to Dharma. Adam and Maya came behind them examining the scene.

"What... happened?" Dharma said, descending on a narrow tongue of old entrance to the glen.

Before her stood an ancient fortress, abandoned, covered in moss and vine, the left wall had completely caved in. Porous, grey, stone enclaves cracking, crumbling into pieces. The structure was grand at one point, covering the entire clearing in the forest. Now it stood in pieces. Near the center grew a sapling clinging to a large granite megalith.

Dharma and Ubuntu sifted through the rubble. Dharma ran her hand along the fallen stone.

"What happened?" Dharma asked, only so it was asked.

Ubuntu gazed into the ruins. A bobcat came out.

"Tjikko can't be..." Dharma started.

"No. Not the mighty Tjikko." Ubuntu said with strength.

"There's only one way to find out," Dharma said, looking at Ubuntu.

The riders navigated through the forest, coming to a cliff at its outer edge. Below, another bowl, full of grey and green, and rising foothills that spiked the landscape.

"There," Dharma said, pointing. "Old Tjikko still stands."

Maya looked out and faintly saw a single fir tree standing in the distance.

"Yes, I see it. I see Tjikko," Maya said.

"Aye. now let's see who is protecting it," Dharma said.

The riders descended one by one from the cliff, to the field leading up to Old Tjikko. Slowly they approached the tree, scanning the landscape, hoping to find some sign of security.

"If Tjikko lives, he would not allow the sacred tree to stand unguarded," Dharma said.

They crouched behind a small cliff, a stone's throw away from Old Tjikko.

"That's the great Old Tjikko?" Adam asked. "It's... I thought it'd be bigger."

"It's called Old Tjikko, not Big Tjikko," Ubuntu said. "Why don't you go up there? Then you'll see the real— big Tjikko."

"Sure, I'll touch the tree," Adam said, getting up to go.

"I don't think you will," Ubuntu said. "But yes, get on with it."

"Maybe I should go," Dharma said.

"Shh, shh," Ubuntu hushed her.

Adam crept out into the open. Stepping onto his board, he slowly and carefully approached. The tree was just a regular old fir, kind of decrepit looking. Adam relaxed his hunched crouch to a slight bend in his back. He drew closer to the tree. He looked back at the other five. He stood up straight, relaxed on gliding, swishing board, and casually approached the inner circle of the tree.

"Guys, its fine!" Adam called back.

"That's not a good thing!" Maya shouted.

Suddenly something swooped in from the sky, and instantly a vicious polar bear came thundering unto the ground, before the tree. Roaring, running rampant, the giant white beast charged at Adam, with slobbering festering jaws.

"Tjikko!" Dharma shouted.

Maya looked at her. Ubuntu cheered.

Adam turned and sprinted. He mounted his board and sped to the group behind the cliff. Ubuntu passed him running. Adam turned in confusion, and continued speeding to safety. Dharma followed close behind Ubuntu, who was running toward the beast. They sprinted at the big white bear. Ubuntu morphed into a Leopard in a happy gallop. Dharma did the same, changing into her snow leopard, and catching up to Ubuntu.

One by one they mauled the bear with joy, and wrestled him unto the ground. The bear roared, and tried to throw the felines off him, but they pounced and bit his neck. He roared in pain, but shortly his roar changed to something different. Some lighter words in the polar bear language.

"Tjikko?" Maya said to Adam.

"I guess that's Tjikko," Adam said, shrugging.

The puppets and the junior riders came out from behind the rock.

The huge bear tossed the little leopards off him turning into less big form of giant man. The leopards did the same.

"Aaaah!" Tjikko said, still roaring. "So good to see my little sisters! Dare I say you've gotten stronger," Tjikko said, rubbing his neck where teeth marks were.

He was a grizzly man, but as a polar grizzly man. Tall, broad, solid, everything. He wore a wild smile that competed with his wild beard for air-time. His hair was long and tangled.

"What on earth happened to your fortress?" Dharma urged, as she gestured in the direction of the forest they just came from.

"Oh, yes, I can explain," Tjikko said. "Well first... we relocated, due west, just inside of Norway. It's prettier. No one ever cares to attack Old Tjikko. We have time to commute"

"About that..." Ubuntu said.

"Or maybe, they never had the balls," Tjikko said. "But anyway, we're undefeated, the elves and me— we can't be beat."

"And the ruins?" Dharma peered.

"Right!" Tjikko, blushed. "Well, we threw a banger of a going away party. So..."

"The place is destroyed," Dharma said, with head held forward, and arms spread wide, "it's literally in ruins."

"They don't call me Tjikko the Great for nothing," Tjikko said.

"Who calls you that?" Ubuntu asked.

"Uh, the elves?" Tjikko said.

"What worthy person calls you that?" Ubuntu said.

"The elves are strong!" Tjikko laughed. "I am strong. Look at the fortress. Come on! Anyways, I couldn't have anyone squatting in the great fortress of Tjikko. It had to be destroyed."

"Come on," Tjikko said. "I'll show you the new fortress; it's more than a fortress, it's a dale."

"I can turn into a coyote," Adam said, proudly, butting in.

"And who is this little guy?" Tjikko asked, standing twice Adam's height.

"Tjikko, this is Adam," Dharma said. "My son."

Tjikko looked at Dharma.

"Your *what*?" he asked, surprised.

"And my Daughter, Maya," Dharma said.

Tjikko looked at Dharma, then Ubuntu. Ubuntu nodded yes.

"It is an absolute pleasure to meet you two," Tjikko said, shaking their hands with his big grimy paw.

"We've heard great things about you Tjikko," Maya said. "Nice to meet you."

"Wait 'til you hear the stuff they left out," Tjikko said. Then he turned to Anastasia and Ignatz "And the yet littler men and women made of wood?"

"Oh, how could I forget," Dharma said. "This is Ignatz."

"How do you do," Ignatz said.

"And Anastasia" Dharma said.

"Nice to meet you," Anastasia said.

"The pleasure is mine," Tjikko said, lowering to her level.

"Well then, it's getting late. Let's get to the valley." Tjikko started walking. He turned, stopping. "So then, where's Zefu?"

"Oh... Tjikko..." Dharma said, bowing her head.

"On his way?" Tjikko asked, trying to have Dharma meet his eyes.

Tjikko looked to Ubuntu with concern.

"It's just a girl's trip?" Tjikko asked, fighting concern.

Ubuntu let her eyes close.

"There is much to catch up on," Dharma said.

So Tjikko led them west. The landscape took an epic turn. Roaming forest cascades turned to towering fjords, turning the landscape into a labyrinth of megalithic rivers, with sheer rock walls majestic, guiding, revealing scenes the eye knows not. Rivers turning layers deeper. Tjikko, leading. Iron giant. Board of double axe heads bedded in a petrified, coarse wood.

"I admit," Dharma said. "This does suit you."

Seven now riders, turn the corner to a river, crooked, leading up the valley. The river found its source from a waterfall at valley's end. Night was falling. Stars. Maya looks around in wonder. The valley glows with golden windows either side that scattered in the stone face. Dwellings hewn in valley sheer, line side walls illuminated. Adam spins. In the walls soft marble sandy columns, decadent patterns.

"Welcome," Tjikko said, floating, "to Dail-Chruim-Puill—the Valley of the Crooked Stream."

<u>Act VI</u>

Chapter 49

The riders floated down the glowing causeway. The river glass below, calm and silent in the night, reflects the navy sky. Elves hovered everywhere, passing each other in the columned hallways carved in valley walls, and crossing in the open air, passing near the riders, smiling. Joyful beings. Like children laughing. The embedded village stretched down both sides of the stone face valley. The golden doors and windows glittered in the night, leading to the waterfall with greatest golden light behind it.

"That's where I stay," Tjikko said, showing them ahead.

The elves bowed as the riders progressed. Tjikko waved to them.

"Just smile and wave," Tjikko said. "They're very conventional beings. Nice, smart, loyal, fierce conventional beings."

The elves were slender men and women wearing almost pure white robes. Fluent in their motion—like they're barely there— they seemed to be one with the still night air. They were riding light-wood boards, like Maya's. They passed each other on the paths, and swirling in the air, trailing in the wake, using pockets leaping such efficient motion.

Tjikko jumped, bluntly falling, scraping a rock, and grunting. He hunkered to a crooked staircase that looked like piano teeth for stairs.

"I did this part," Tjikko said proudly.

"I see that," Dharma smiled.

The stairs beside the water fall led up and back into the rock. The light shines through the falling water, giving it the look of falling light.

"Let's get you some food," Tjikko said.

Tjikko led them up the set of meandering stairs to the façade of a three-story chateau in the blue stone wall. At ground level was a set of grand, dark, hardwood gates embedded in the cliff. The gates opened heavily into the rough stone walls of the first floor of the building, and the disappearing staircase which they climbed. Above, the gate a sweeping semi-circle arc of broad, sandstone balcony lined with marble-wooden banister, leads into a glowing egress. The group poured forth from the spiral staircase onto shining, marble floors 'neath arching hallway ceiling bright and warm. Corridors branch out, corner, leading deep into the bedrock of the fjord.

The final level was a narrower floor. There were a few yellow windows, flickering with an added orange fire lit from within. Outside, a balcony smaller than the one below, encircles the room. This was Tjikko's quarters, the eagles landing, nested beneath the overhang of rock that was the mouth of the cascading waterfall.

Tjikko carried dinner plates, assisted by two elves, with plates full of potatoes, vegetables and meat. The group of riders gathered at a table prepared on the terrace of the balcony.

Dharma and the group inform Tjikko of their toils and their struggle, the details leading up to now: How Zeddefungo stumbled upon Maya and Adam lost in the woods; the battles with the Dark Boards and their factions; the death of

Zeddefungo; the reunion of Dharma and Ubuntu; the rescue of Adam; and the plan of the sinister Radu.

"None of this is free," Tjikko said, setting down his plate. "It's all running around, fighting, preparing and fearing. In rising to meet the Dark Boards their reign has already begun."

"What do you expect us to do?" Dharma asked. "Allow them to take complete control of the planet? They intend to choke the life from the world, and leave a gray and withering earth."

"I know," Tjikko said. "I have fought them for centuries. I have seen their nature."

"Yes, we have fought them together." Dharma said. "We have all seen the black hole in the place of their heart. That is why we must exterminate them— Tjikko, what do you mean?"

"Balance, freedom, what the universe has intended—" Tjikko said, as he looked into the waterfall. "Balance is not pushing back against an evil force."

"Surely balance is not— surrendering," Ubuntu replied, confused.

"I have fought the Dark Boards for centuries," Tjikko said. "I have roamed these northern hills for ages. They have spoken to me. Consider for a moment the land. It multiplies, and unfolds exponentially as you enter and seek. But we are to forget the land, to turn and fight—"

"Yes, to ensure that land exists to explore!" Dharma exclaimed.

"How powerful can the Dark Boards truly be?" Tjikko asked. "In the beginning free was free. Then yes, they turned, and they tampered with the balance out of pride, and they used the creation, the creatures. How powerful can they truly be? They prey on a select few, relatively."

Tjikko walked over to the balcony.

"They prey on millions through the years— billions!" Dharma said. "And even if it was one soul it wouldn't matter. It would be our duty to ensure that soul was safe. Tjikko, what has happened to you in these hills? They killed Zeddefungo, your brother."

"They feed on our resistance," Tjikko said.

"That's not true," Ubuntu said. "You are to say that they would sit complacent if we pulled away?"

"That's not what I'm saying," Tjikko said. "I don't know what the right course is."

"Well you've run out of time," Ubuntu said. "And I think your perspective is out of touch, up here at the top of the world."

"Well, where is the Father of Boards? What is his perspective?" Tjikko exclaimed. "I would not let one hair be harmed on one child's head if I had the power, but it has been the same idea time and time again, this conflict...this conflict. It won't be won by one side stamping out the other. That is not balance. That is volleying."

Tjikko stood beside the railing of the balcony. "I'm more than convicted with anger toward the Dark Boards, more so now that they have taken my beloved— *deeply*— my brother," Tjikko said. "My brother... But this is deeper than the battle for the earth. The thousandth battle for the earth. In light of what I've seen, what I heard from you tonight, my sisters... I will fight. But I will no longer be a slave to death."

Dharma and Ubuntu looked at each other.

"It is not the Dark Boards I am fighting," Tjikko said. "It is the threat of death, they hold over us and the entire population, with their tendrils. I tell you, that is the extent of their power. But I am free."

Ubuntu and Dharma sat for a moment.

"That is right my brother," Ubuntu said. "And, I am free too."

"And I am with you," Dharma said. "There is no end."

"That is right," Tjikko said, leaning large paws of hands on his sisters' shoulders, in a hugging gesture. "Therefore, the only death there really is, is to live without freedom."

"The way it was— has been," enjoined Ubuntu.

Adam and Maya sat ensconced, not moving since the onset of the discourse.

"So, I'm confused, are we fighting, or...?" Adam asked, taking a bite of his potatoes.

"We will ride, we will fight, we will win," Tjikko answered. "But we will ride their evil forces like the waves of a storm-filled ocean."

"Is that good?" Maya asked.

"My favorite time to ride," Ubuntu said.

"We have to win, you know," Maya said. "'Cuz there are billions of people, who are *not* centuries old, and *haven't* seen the beginning of time, let alone this conversation, and they are very afraid of dying."

"Right," Tjikko said. "Yes, but on another level, it matters not whether they believe it, one way or the other. They will arrive with us all one day, riding and living free through the waves of eternity."

"Yeah," Maya said. "Well, keep that level to yourself okay?"

"Sure, yes, respect the journey," Tjikko said. "But you get it right?" He said, pointing at Maya.

"I don't know, I think you barely 'get it,'" Maya said, with air quotes.

"I like this girl," Tjikko said. "Truly, so much like her mother." Tjikko slapped his hand on the table. "It's getting late; let's get you all a place to sleep for the night. –Bella?" he called.

One of the elves helping with the plates stepped forward. She appeared to be Maya and Adam's age, slightly taller than Maya, with fair skin and hair and darker blue eyes.

"Yes, Tjikko?" the elf asked.

"Can you show everyone to an area where they can sleep and get situated?" Tjikko asked.

"Of course," Bella said, looking to the group.

"Maya, Adam, how would you like to visit Tjikko with me in the morning— second watch, nothing crazy." Tjikko asked.

"Aye," Adam said, tipping an imaginary hat.

Tjikko looked aside to Dharma, slightly confused. Dharma shrugged smiling.

"Yes, we'd love to," Maya said.

"Wonderful," Tjikko said. "Now, let's get some rest."

Bella took them out to a more neatly crafted staircase, stemming from the side of the castle, as it rose and curved towards the quarters of the elves.

Maya and Adam followed as Bella led them into the main hallway within the rock wall. A small aqueduct brought clear water, through the lamplit tunnel, in a little trough. The elves came and collected bowls and cups from the water flow.

"I like our new dwelling much better than the last," Bella confessed. "We elves have been around almost as long as Tjikko."

"The dwelling is beautiful," Adam said, behind Bella. "About how long are we talking though?"

"Well, I'm 300,000 years old," Bella said. "We elves reach back to Tjikko's infancy, when he befriended our grandfather, before time began to crystallize," Bella said.

They took a turn into the mountain, down a labyrinth— half hallway, half living quarters— geometrically stacked, artistically ornamented, all open, and all bright.

"The world was so much different," Bella said spiritedly. "There were many, many more elves that rode the hills—a blooming high culture in the north! Of course, we can still communicate with consciousness— and we don't even need to eat!"

"We don't eat either!" Ignatz said. "Maybe we are elves," he said to Anastasia.

Dharma smiled at Ubuntu. The group of riders followed Bella down between the corners and quarters of rooms, with ledges and open windows that were beige and mostly smooth, but maintaining signs of handmade craftsmanship.

"Here we go!" Bella said. "A few open cubes, or squares or rooms or something. I don't know, I'm better at thinking my talking to you."

She looked at another elf girl nearby and flashed a message to her.

"Yes, of course they can stay here," the other woman said. "These are extra dorms. Let me get you all some blankets and some pillows. Elf silk," she said, aside. "Sewn from reindeer belly fur spun with mountain mist."

"Yes," Adam said, sleepily.

And everybody laid down dozing, after taking off their bags and boards, and placing them in corners. They talked a little into the night, in the warm beige light of the caverns.

Chapter 50

Tjikko, Maya and Adam arrived at Old Tjikko, decelerating in the thick, early-morning fog. The old tree stood distinguished and solitary on the mountaintop. There was an aura in its presence, as if it were surrounded by some crowd. Yet, the land nearby was barren. Shrubby grass, grey gravel and scraggy rocks. Almost flattened in its appearance.

Tjikko looked upon the tree with reverence and nonchalance. The towering old pine was slightly crooked in its age. It's branches and needles merged with lichen, like some kind of semi-aquatic tree.

"The greatest of the great trees!" Tjikko said. He took some steps around the tree. "The Tree of Time," he said, and it pulled his eyebrows up in awe and reverie, "S/he has seen the climb and descent of generations, like waves on the sea."

"It's not even that big," Adam whispered to Maya.

"Planted by the Father of Boards himself. Given unto me to protect," said Tjikko, patting the bark of the tree with respect. "An old friend."

Maya looked around into the mist in the surrounding foothills. The lines of moisture blew slowly in the valley below.

"—Uncle Tjikko?" Adam asked.

"Uncle *what*?" Tjikko asked.

"Nothing," Adam said. "I just wanted to call you that. Let's kill some Dark Boards! I'm getting hungry!"

"Right." Tjikko said, agreeing. "Well, Syv and Ullr are on the lookout. Syv in the south, Ullr in the north. They are twin brothers, the fastest elves alive."

"I'm positive I could beat them," Adam said.

"No," Tjikko said. "This is different speed."

"I'm fast." Adam said.

"He is surprisingly fast," Maya said.

"Well, maybe you can race," Tjikko said. "Regardless, when the brothers give the word, we will ride. But until then, just enjoy the mountain air."

So, Adam sat and threw rocks around. And Maya examined Old Tjikko, running her fingers across the worn bark, looking up into its wispy, ghosts of branches.

"Can we go?" Adam asked. "Maybe the Dark Boards changed their mind. Lost their nerve, you know?" He chucked a rock into the valley. "Do you think Bella likes me?"

"No," Tjikko and Maya said, simultaneously.

"Ah, what do you guys know?" Adam said. "I need my dawgs, Jatta and Nicu. Where are they anyway? They would know what I'm talking about. Although, Bella might be fond of Jatta. Come to think of it, maybe it'd be better if they didn't get here either. No, Jatta's got a thing for Maya."

"What?" Maya startled.

"What? Oh, come on Maya," Adam said.

"—Quiet," Tjikko said suddenly, putting out his hand.

Maya and Adam listened searching for what Tjikko was listening for. Faint at first, but a distant horn of three-note melody came, and came swiftly over the hills.

In an instant, with a gust of wind, an elf was there before them on his board. He was fierce and fair, with orange-brown eyes, full of alarm at the moment.

"Syv, my boy, what is it?" Tjikko asked.

"Riders approaching— from the south— in the hundreds, sir!" Syv said, breathing heavily.

Tjikko weighed the situation.

"Syv, get to the fjord," Tjikko commanded.

"Yes, sir," Syv responded.

"Prepare the warriors— we need a team around the tree— immediately," Tjikko said. "Maya and Adam, come with me," Tjikko said, turning.

"They come by way of the great valley," Syv said, handing Tjikko a brass telescope. With that Syv sped off in a flash.

"Come," Tjikko said. "We will do what we can to stall them. The three of us spread out, attack the hooded leaders, hope the impacted command will trip the soldiers up."

Tjikko bolted into the sky, followed by Maya and Adam. They barreled through the hills, in the timeless grey noon. They came upon the mountain walls of the great, snaking valley.

Tjikko took cover behind a ridge in the trees.

"There," Tjikko said, looking out. Several flying V's of riders soared through the skies, with five riders at the helm.

Tjikko extended the telescope and scouted out the ranks.

"This is it," Tjikko said. "Let me take the brunt of it. If I go down, fall back and join the others." Tjikko handed Maya the telescope to have a look.

"I'll go out with a bang that's for sure, buy you some time," Tjikko said. "I estimate I could take down a good hundred riders. Should I just lead with that?"

"No Unc'. We can't have another Boardsmen sacrifice themselves for us— bunch of martyrs!" Adam said. "It's all or nothing this time."

Maya was looking through the telescope. She took it down and looked. Then put it up again to see.

"It was an honor to have met you both," Tjikko said, bowing. "I'll see you on the other side, one way or another." With that he bolted forth from their position, screaming toward the riders.

"Tjikko wait!" Maya screamed. "I don't see any hoods."

Adam snatched the telescope.

"That's *not* hoods. That's— wood!" Adam said.

He blasted out with force that blew the trees back knocking Maya over. He tore through the air catching Tjikko just in time.

"Tjikko! Tjikko!!" Adam yelled.

Confused at how Adam caught him, nevertheless Tjikko pulled back on the reigns.

"It's Tzara! And the Tree of Life!" Adam yelled, hooting as they came in contact with the riders.

Tjikko stared. And his confusion turned to sheer joy.

"Kazzo!" Tjikko yelled to Jatta's father.

"Tjikko! It's been too long!" Kazzo said, embracing him. "Truly too long!"

The riders gave a big fat bear hug. Hundreds of warriors and puppet warriors flooded the sky. Seven massive flying V's arranged now halted, suspended in the air.

"You did it, Tzara!" said Adam. "You really did it."

"We did more than 'it', my friend. We brought the whole Bohemia with us!" Tzara exclaimed.

Maya flew in, joining the reunion.

"Tzara! Jaccapo! What a relief!" said Maya. "How did you even—"

"Eh, we took the scenic route and flew by night," Tzara said. "You know, the usual."

The wooden colorful riders were dispersed among the fierce painted warriors of the Tree of Life. A diverse crew but surprisingly they seemed to be getting on quite well, with laughter and good cheer, jests and brotherhood, sisterhood rolling through the crowd.

"Thank you, Tzara," Maya said.

"Aghem," Jaccapo coughed.

"And where would Tzara be without you, good Jaccapo?" Maya said, realizing.

"Probably in a big grass nest, in the bosom of his new, silverback, big-mama gorilla," Jaccapo stated.

"Mmm, Pinocchio-Tarzan." Adam said, concluding.

"Huh?" said Jaccapo.

"Nothing, I'll show you later," Adam said.

"Maya!" Jatta shouted from the side.

He flew to her, and hugged her, and sent them spinning.

"You're alive!" said Jatta, holding her shoulders.

Nicu and Adam gave a handshake hug.

"Jatta, my boy." said Tjikko, entering. "How old are you now?"

"325,000, sir," Jatta said, smiling wide.

"Incredible! 10 teraseconds?" Tjikko said, putting a big hand on his shoulder. "Last time I saw you, you were kicking around a baby board."

Adam swung up, and around, and looked out over the floating crowds.

"Wow! These are some numbers!" Adam said, elated.

Tjikko floated up with Jatta's dad.

"Let's get back to the fjord and bring this good news to the group," Tjikko said. "What a ray of hope. United, we will be peeling those greedy, ugly demons off the bottoms of our boards in no time. Come! This calls for a feast!"

"Yes, let's get out of here before the real Dark Boards arrive," Adam said.

Kazzo put his arm around Tjikko, and the miscellaneous assembly of rider-warriors proceeded west toward the Valley of the Crooked Stream, soon to become double in the mix-matched nature of their armies.

Chapter 51

Tjikko and the swarm of riders came within a stone's throw of the team that was now protecting the Great Tree.

"I'll go ahead before good Syv gives the orders on us," Tjikko said. He sped forward and descended before a stiff Syv. Behind Syv the team of thirty elves stood ready for imminent battle, ready to defend.

"Good Syv," Tjikko said.

Syv floated, tense, full of nerve to fight for his life.

"At ease, good Syv," Tjikko said. "The riders you saw were not Dark Boards."

From below the riders glided up the hill in promising numbers. The nerve in Syv washed clean, and he let out a deep breath.

"At ease!" Syv said, turning to his team.

The elves let go of their poised, crouched posture and rose, standing plainly. As the myriad riders climbed the hill, the small team of elves exchanged good looks of joy and vigor.

Tjikko smiled warmly to present them.

"I give you, the soldiers of the Tree of Life, and our new friends, and allies, the puppets from— Bohemia?" Tjikko said, turning to the puppets. "Where are you guys from?"

"Sure," Tzara said, incredibly boldly.

The rest of the army glided up to meet the group of elves. Tzara shook the hand of Syv. The whole of them were determined and topped with confidence.

"Come, if we are given this night, it will be spent in feast." Tjikko said, hospitably. "Syv, good Syv. Sorry, will have to take your plate to the southern watch. The Dark Boards could come at any time."

"Yes, of course," Syv said. "I will harken the feast of our victory."

"That is why we call you good Syv," Tjikko said, as he gave a nod, with a hand on Syv's shoulder.

The party, 400 strong, arrived at the fjord. They rounded the corner of the mountains steep and glided slowly into the Valley of the Crooked Stream. One elf, in the corridor, was the first to see them. She dropped her vase of water in her alarm, which transformed to pure exuberant awe.

"Tjikko has returned!" she turned and screamed to the others.

The message spread like fire through the halls. Slowly the elves emerged to realize Tjikko was not alone. Upon seeing these reinforcements, they stormed and crowded the open ledges of the corridors.

The puppets and the soldiers of the Tree of Life were teeming with pride. The scene was full of jubilation. The elves came out to meet the riders. All were greeted, reunited and introduced to one another. Spirits were at an all-time high.

Ubuntu and Dharma joined the crew. Anastasia and Ignatz tackled Jaccapo and Tzara.

"Tzara," Dharma said. "You over-achiever!"

"That is one ruthless puppet!" Kazzo reflected to the group.

Ubuntu found her husband and embraced him.

"Numo," she cried. "It has been too long, too long."

Tjikko couldn't keep his head still or his arms down. He took in the reunion of the riders in the center of the fjord.

"I love company," Tjikko said. "—Windermere! Bella!"

Bella appeared with a disheveled elven man who was Tjikko's right hand man.

"Come, help me prepare the feast," Tjikko said. "Clear the cellar of the finest food. The finest everything!" Tjikko said. "For this feast could well be our last!"

Chapter 52

To the east, across the black Gulf of Brothia, a droning hum. The soldiers of the Dark Boards march bleakly permeating the landscape. This quad ruled grid of death chokes the northern brown-red earth. The metal soldiers are variations, shades of dull, gray, iridescent, purple, navy, mauve. They mow down the curvature of the earth. They fade into the light of early evening, neither light nor dark, only swallowing the profiles, playing tricks with the silhouettes of the ranks in the nihilism sky.

Radu perches with his right- and left-hand man, Arthur and Dracul, on a high cliff to oversee the herd. Giant birds of black smoke circle and screech in whispers.

"The world will be so beautiful, clothed in the garments of our ways," Radu said. "It is as if Mother Earth is asking us to bring forth this new era, by delivering us this boy. Nudging us to rid the earth of the funk and over growth it has endured, and usher in this change it wants— this logical step in evolution! Do you feel it? Do you here her call?"

"Yes, my Lord, I hear it," Arthur answers.

"The Boardsmen imagine that they are preserving the harmony of the planet, when the earth is the anomaly in the universe," Radu said. "It burns with fire green and vibrant, blue and luminous. More deadly a habitat has never been seen! These devils, rightly called, believe they are angels!"

Radu drew near to the edge.

"No more," Radu said. "We will restore the planet to its true glory. A glory only darker minds can understand. A setting only darker vision can perceive. Until the ultimate darkness is reached. Praise Darkness!"

Suddenly one of the black smoke vultures flew too close to the ranks of soldiers, knocking one into the other. Tempers flared. The soldier manned his board and retaliated against the giant vulture. Soon the fighting drew in other vultures and soldiers, like a vortex, until a large portion of the ranks had fallen into fighting.

Two or three of the hoods tried to break up the fighting. Finally, Radu himself stormed in and burst forth with red rays of light, holding the perpetrators frozen in the air. With a hook and a twist of his board, he drove them deep into the earth and buried them.

"Will there be any other hissy fits?" Radu screamed tensely, as he looked around at the grimacing metal men.

"I thought the soldiers weren't supposed to show emotion," Dracul said to Arthur, the two remaining high on distant cliff.

"A spell bears the finger prints of its executioner," Arthur shrugged.

Radu returned to the cliff fuming.

"Is there a problem here?" Radu asked furiously.

"No problem my Lord," Arthur said.

"No," Dracul said.

"Good!" Radu replied, brushing off his cloak. "We will reach Tjikko at sun up. As you can see our men are chomping at the bit. We need to get the right bit in front of them to chomp on."

Radu clapped his clammy clear palms.

"Get my carrier" Radu said. "I must enjoy my final night of rest, as a measly ruler of the shadows. Tomorrow we bring the shadows to the world."

Dracul and Arthur harnessed Radu's carrier. The carrier was a canvas tent on floating boards. Several soldiers in the ranks protected it in the middle of the pack. They followed behind and laid on boards themselves, as soldiers marched into the evening.

The light fades. The heard presses on. It bores forth a path, with Tjikko in its sights. It blankets the foothills in its grid, as far as eyes can see, and disappears into the night, screeching, churning, breathing— nameless.

Chapter 53

At the fjord, dogs burst through doors of the great hall, tongues flapping, bodies wrestling. The hall swelling with a roar of jubilant sound. Long tables extended it seemed endlessly into the hollow mountain. The finger of the fjord mountain was scalloped and hollow, filled with windows. In the middle, tables full of food forever. Meats, fruits, potatoes, vegetables, stews, casseroles, pies, cakes, more meat, and a full moose roast. Tjikko doesn't mess around.

The puppets, the elves, and the jungle warriors commingle across the room. Boarders ride beneath the high towering ceiling, back and forth and chasing. An elf quartet in the corner had turned to a bohemian jungle symphony and jams the night away. Ballads, rags, and tribal ceremony music fused and feeding on the atmosphere, sweeping the feast into the stars above.

Adam slaps his tin plate down, overflowing with feast food. He takes his seat at the table. Utensils clanked on plates the room around.

"Hello, children's table," Adam says.

Maya, Bella, Jatta, Nicu, Ignatz, Anastasia, Jaccapo and Tzara sat in brilliantly warming conversation underneath the golden lamps that hang above the tables.

"I am no child," Tzara says.

"No Tzara, not you! You should be promoted to a real boy!" Adam jested.

"What is all this talk of real boys in relation to us puppets?" Tzara asked, sort of going along.

"It's nothing," Maya answered. "Maybe just, try not to lie, and check for your father in a giant whale."

"What? That is oddly insensitive," Tzara answered.

"Sorry, sorry," Maya said. "It's Pinocchio."

"Yes, my cousin. His name is Pinocchio. He's over there," Tzara answered. "What about him?"

"No, the story— wait, what?" Maya said.

"Okay you guys have fun," Tzara said. "I'm going to sit at the adult human table where they will respect me as the hero that I am."

Maya and Adam looked at each other. Maya grimaced trying not to laugh.

Anastasia sat by Adam making little houses with her food.

"Don't worry about Tzara," Anastasia said. "He was made without a funny bone."

Adam waited, to see if she was kidding. Anastasia smiled.

"What an incredible place," Jatta says, while stuffing his face with food. "What an incredible night, with incredible people." He says, as his gaze is directed towards Maya.

Maya blushes.

"If there is any chance that we are to die soon, I am so grateful to have met you all," Jatta says

"No chance," Adam says, eating cake. "We're getting out of here alive. Then we're gonna ride together to the ends of the earth, exploring, looking for sweet spots."

"Speaking of a sweet spot," Maya said to Adam, as he crammed some chocolate cake into his mouth. "You got a little..." Maya pointed to his cheek.

Anastasia dabs his cheek a little with her napkin. They share a moment.

Maya looks a little confused for a second, but reels, in her continuing discrimination of the puppets.

"Adam," Bella says softly. "Can you show me that amazing trick again?" she asks. "The one where you flip your board around beneath your feet?"

"The kickflip?" Adam asks.

"Yes, that's the one," Bella answers.

"Sure," Adam said. "You guys really don't go for style points up here in elf land, do you?"

They walk away, and Anastasia hangs her head a little.

At the grownups table, Tjikko scarves down plate after plate of hearty food. Dharma looks on in slight distaste.

"You just watch," Tjikko says. "You'll be hungry tomorrow. I'm telling you. When I come in and save you from Radu, you can thank the extra pork chops."

"Yes, brother," Dharma answers. "I have thanked the pork chops many times. If it weren't for them I wouldn't be here. Remember Lake Baykal?" she says, enlightening.

"Siberia?" Tjikko said. "Yes of course. You can thank the beef stew for that one. I brought a pouch specifically for battle on that mission.

"Well, they sure don't call you Tjikko the slender," Ubuntu interjected.

"That's right, they don't. They call me—Tjikko the Great." He stood in mock glory.

"Great gut." Ubuntu said.

"This is nice," Dharma said, looking out at all the action. All the good men and women were laughing, loving, and living.

"I wouldn't have it any other way" says Tjikko.

The music fills the hall and through the corridors. Bella and Adam stand alone looking out a big tall window in the hallway. Windermere pokes his head out looking back and forth.

"Bellaaa," he calls. "Tjikko's looking for you. Saying something of bringing out the special cheese."

"What?" Bella replied. "We never use the special cheese."

"He said break the glass and bring it out here," Windermere insisted.

Bella looked at Adam and instructed him to stay there; and she would be right back. And then she fled back into the ballroom, down a stairwell.

Anastasia stands behind Windermere. She high fives him and goes to Adam standing in the moonlight of the corridor.

"It's beautiful isn't it?" Anastasia asks, looking up at the moon.

"It is," says Adam as he turned to look at Anastasia.

She reaches up and kisses him, standing on her tippy toes, grabbing Adam's collar and pulling up to him for a long kiss. Adam looks into her eyes.

"In case we're gonna die you know," Anastasia says.

"Yeah," Adam says, with his arms around her.

In the ballroom, Ignatz sits alone with Nicu.

"You can do what?" Nicu says.

"I can turn invisible," Ignatz answers. "I just think of a cat, and then poof I'm gone."

Outside, in the clear night air Jatta walks with Maya on the open walkway riverside.

"You look— really nice," Jatta said, eyes cast down, then looking up at Maya.

"You're crazy," Maya said. "I haven't brushed my hair in months."

"Well I like it," Jatta flirted.

"When this is over, maybe we can... I don't know... go to dinner together?" Jatta proposed. "I don't know how to do this. You're a city girl. I literally live in a tree."

Maya turned in front of him, came in close, and looked up into his eyes.

"I would love to," Maya said. She gave him a long kiss.

Jatta held her hand and walked with love in his step from head to toe. Maya laid her head on his shoulder. She had forgotten about the whole world, the whole war. She was simply walking slowly on the water, still as glass. They sat beneath the moon on wooden bench and threw out little pebbles making little splashes with concentric ripples.

"I've never seen a girly like you," Jatta said.

Maya melted in his arms. They hugged each other close and thought of nothing. The night sky undulated in the ripples on the fjord.

The people in the ballroom looked into each other's eyes with pure emotion. Some of them had never met until tonight. But in each other's eyes, they found a ground of being. The jubilee and even love had dwindled into something more, a radiance beyond words. A pure transcendent understanding no one knew was possible until this setting. Still the closest word for this is love.

Chapter 54

An empty tin cup fell from the fingers of a sleeping hand, echoing in the quiet hall. The feet of two dogs clicked on the stone floor, as they searched from plate to plate for scraps. Through the windows cast a pale, metallic, blue light of early dawn.

The elves made room for the warriors. The latter and the puppets lie dispersed throughout the rooms stacked within the valley walls. All strewn and sprawled, sleeping heavily from a good night's feast.

Maya came to the railing of the valley wall in the brisk morning air. A cold wind rolled over the waterfall and down the fjord from the north. Maya peered into the breeze.

Tjikko rolled over in his watchtower bed, kingly room, windows open to the crescent moon, through cascading water, losing its yellow glow of night.

Just then, with a whirlwind, Ullr was on the terrace, with an urgent air.

"Ullr, my boy," Tjikko said, sitting up.

"Tjikko." Ullr said, breathing heavily. "It's Radu. —The Dark Boards –Passing through the Lapponian gate as we speak."

"So, they are," Tjikko said, standing up at once and throwing on his boots.

He grabbed his ax-board from the wall.

"Spread the word," Tjikko said. "Everyone. Assemble in the fjord immediately."

There was grabbing of boards and boots throughout the quarters. All were poised. There was a laser like focus in the air.

Adam handed Maya her board.

"We've come so far sis," Adam said "No way we're going down now."

"No way," Maya said. "They will pay for what they did to you," she grabbed his shoulders. "Good luck out there."

"You say it like I'd ever leave your side," Adam said.

A smile forced its way up into Maya's bottom lip with pride.

"You raised them right," Ubuntu said to Dharma sliding on her boots.

"They did it by themselves," Dharma sighed, with love.

"Yes, and so you raised them right," Ubuntu said, pointing to Dharma's heart. "Even if from somewhere else."

The warriors gathered in the fjord, filling the valley with their numbers. Loose clothing fluttered in the breeze. The sea of riders floated, outlined against a blue-grey sky. Tjikko levitated at the helm.

"Riders!" He pierced the silence of the morning. "Today... we fight... for Zeddefungo —for freedom! —for Earth!"

The riders roared like nobody was watching. Dharma and Ubuntu hovered at Tjikko's side.

"Today!" Tjikko continued, "We remove the lie of fear —restore the clarity of reality!"

"For the babies," Dharma whispered.

"We do it for all the babies!" Tjikko shouted, "Who see it clear and pure!"

The warriors roared again, rocking on their boards within the crowd. Energy rising in the solution, with Tjikko's words the solvent.

"We ride—" Tjikko shouted, "for the head of the beast!!"

He screamed in fury and riders cascaded over the walls of the fjord, north to the mountains. And north the riders flew, crossing over fjords and mountains, high lakes and endless pine forest.

Maya looked out to the west where the sea was visible, and the dim cold sky mixed with the iron sea of the same, no horizon to speak of. To the east she saw the sun peaking over the land, rising toward the cloud line. Soon it would be swallowed by the overcast dome.

The riders looked upon the burst of sunrise in stoic meditation. There was a fullness of presence in the soldiers. They were one, united, —mind, body, and soul extended into numbers. The pack, the pride, the herd, but more so like a deadly school of fish— Piranhas, or a swarm of killer bees.

The sun slipped behind the dome of clouds, and in the distance the enemy came into view, appearing numerous and dark, as their grid blanketed the hills.

The Metallic soldiers slowed their march to a halt in the mountains. The black smoke birds with dark electric wings flapped and hovered over the forces. They came to rest in a broad valley, facing Tjikko and the riders.

Radu and Tjikko, Dharma and Ubuntu with the lesser hooded figures, rise before the warring armies, poised and buzzing with highest frequencies summoned. Spirit of war summoning forms inaccessible until signals are given.

Face to face they float in bright grey sky, fluttered cloaks in wind.

"This is your last chance, Radu!" Tjikko yelled. "Call your men off and come with us. We will make use of you. Your only punishment will be to watch the peaceful prosper of the world."

The riders hovered in the shadow of Tjikko— elves, puppets, jungle Warriors— fronted by Maya and Adam. The motley forces were a valiant effort in the face of the metallic army of the Dark Boards, but ultimately a pale comparison to their numbers.

"I only offer you all a similar fate," Radu Hisses. "Join me, and I will sap your power— drain your souls, yes, but leave you alive to finally come to the realization that the Dark Boards are the future, the logical evolution of the universe."

"You are the worst Radu," Tjikko said. "And somehow even worse than I remember, with your new little crew you've got behind you."

"And you're the same old Tjikko: Fat and destined to lose," Radu said.

And with that, Tjikko launched into the attack that started the battle.

The riders burst forth screaming across the valley. The metallic soldiers mounted their boards robotically and blasted off across the valley. The puppets, the jungles, the bird's electric— the masses came together with an enormous crash of flesh and wood and metal. Puppets exploded upon contact.

"We'll take the birds then!" Tzara yelled. "Yes! Puppets will work on the birds!"

Riders were swooping down with crossing blows. The air was filled with a mad frenzy of fighting. Jatta dodged a blow, swooping in with power, dodging one more soldier, smashing down the back of metal moron's head. The attack was not as critical as Jatta had hoped. The solid soldier took the blow and came for Jatta in the air.

The jungle fighters, with heavy boards and bodies, had some luck with deliberate, forceful board attacks. The elves attempted their initial board attacks, but resorted to more strategic methods.

Three elves came through from one direction—pink!-pink!-pink! Another three elves came across other way, a deadly 'X'— critical hit. But this was six to one in ratio, whereas one metallic soldier took out six elf riders by himself.

Adam fled the clutches of three Dark Boarders chasing through the battle. Adam led them through a cliff hole in the nearby mountains. With one maneuver sent them crashing into rocks, and Maya came and finished with a smashing flatten powered by her board.

"Now that's what I call teamwork!" Adam remarked.

Dharma and Ubuntu, back to back, send bands of orange and yellow light into the dark attacking masses, streaming in on them from all directions. Sending orange and yellow lasers saving those in need.

Tjikko singled out Radu. The feeling was mutual. The Viking and the faceless white hood rose above the battle.

They blasted toward each other with supersonic imminence. The white-hot impact emitted an almost digital explosive ion ring of energy. Tjikko tipped the scales and started driving on Radu. Radu began to gouge Tjikko's eyes and bite his bicep, tearing at his flesh. Tjikko, spinning to the earth, now threw Radu six feet down into the ground following, smashing him into the crater, milling through the earth with bolts of energy thrashing through the dirt.

In spite of Tjikko, Dharma and Ubuntu's efforts, the forces of the Dark Boards moved like a violent glacier, scraping the armies of the Boardsmen from the earth.

"They're just too heavy!" Adam shouted, seeing his army starting to come apart at the seams.

"Resist!" Tzara screamed, flying by on the back of a bird.

Twenty puppets labored on the black beast, smoking, bolting blue electric.

"Rip it's neck out!" Tzara shouted to the crew.

They pulled on the beast's wings and beat its back until it flew into the ground crashing, dying, final bolts of blue like sparks emitting. Nearby riders cheering. Tzara and the puppets out for blood, jumping on the backs of other birds and biting them.

Tjikko sees the army pushing down on them. Fighting Radu, he slashes a spinning, enlarging board of bright green light through the crowd of metal soldiers, mowing down a region.

Radu hisses yet again.

"The Boardsmen, you worthless gimps, target the Boardsmen!" Radu shouts at the lesser hoods. "They are the only thing standing between us and the tree!"

Arthur and Dracul enclosed on Dharma and ubuntu whittling away at the forces of the metal soldiers.

"I'm going to have to ask you to stop that!" Dracul charged.

Ubuntu fielded his attack. She fell back, caught him with her board and sent him crashing at the wall of a nearby cliff. She smashed a ball of bright orange light in his direction.

"I'll deal with both of you." Arthur said, rising slowly, summoning white ghost powers. A phantom aura surrounded him.

"Somebody's been stealing from the cookie jar of siphoned spirit." Dharma said. "You know, that's my son's power you're wearing, there. You should really give it back!"

Dharma sent a disk of yellow light, her board spinning madly at Dracul. Ubuntu charged. The phantom aura disembodied itself and caught Dharma's attack, but Ubuntu bull rushed full-force into the phantom gut, through the spectre, into Arthur, driving him into a tree trunk, planting on his body, sending Dharma back her board.

"Thanks sis," Dharma said.

Elsewhere, the Tjikko-Radu matchup continues. Radu pulverizes Tjikko, flat on his back, into a rocky hillside, sending carnage into the air. Tjikko bench presses Radu's board from his chest.

"You killed my brother!" Tjikko screams in rage. "I don't care about your plans! I don't care about your war! I want you dead!"

Tjikko lands two crossing blows, knocking back the hood revealing Radu's silicone skin, oozing fresh black and purple blood. Radu wiped the blood from his face, looking at it on his fingers.

"I will personally escort you to your brother soon enough." Radu said. "You can join him in the bottomless black pit that is the void of no return! And you can burn for a thousand years on your way down!" screamed Radu, with guttural yell and power coming from a different place.

He lashed out at Tjikko, beaming white lightning from his board. Tjikko caught Radu's lightning with a cracking green light. They countered board attacks, climbing high above the battle once more.

Dharma and Ubuntu looked up at Tjikko and Radu, locked in battle. The air around them began to form a vortex, dark, swirling slow, and changing directions. They were sending their boards flying, throwing, kicking white and green eruptions, blowing out the darkness and coming crashing back, and pressing in, locking in a stalemate, light coming from their boards.

The war raged on below. Soldiers of the Dark Boards gaining, gaining momentum, absorbing weak attacks like nothing. The unstoppable force grinded throughout the mountains, leaving a trail of soldiers of the Boardsmen in its path. The metallic army pressed on southward, encroaching on Old Tjikko territory.

Above, Radu got a hold of Tjikko and began to spin. The revolutions began to glow in red and white and black and suddenly he launched Tjikko, sending him across the landscape landing in a trough and finally a crater.

"Fall back!" Ubuntu shouted to her waning forces. "Regroup!"

The riders climbed behind the ravines inside the mountainsides. The Dark Boards continued, assuming grid position again.

Radu wiped the blood from both his cheeks. He was smiling a nasty grin with, bright black eyes fixed ahead. His generals joined his side and removed their black hoods, revealing porcelain skin and bright red eyes. Dracul began to snicker.

Behind cover, Maya and Ubuntu sat with Dharma, watching them advance like a magma.

"They're just too heavy," Adam panted. "Tjikko's dead."

"Will you stop saying they're too heavy," Maya answered. "Tjikko's not dead. I see him twitching."

"What are we gonna do?" Adam asked.

"We will fight," Ubuntu said. "We will win."

"Where is the science behind that?" Adam cried.

"Stay in the moment," Dharma said "Fight to the very last drop. As long as I have sight, I will fight, with all my might. --All my might, my Adam."

Maya, mesmerized by war or fighting, gazes wide eyed at the battle. The scattered riders of her side, performing acts of valor, squashed into the mud. The puppets flung off birds and were electrocuted. She looks at huddled riders on the hill side, breathing heavily, catching their breath.

She holds her board and looking down begins to see a picture in her mind: her dad, her family, on a sunny day inside their house. Her mom is home. The white curtains blowing in the breeze, the green grass outside. Everything is perfect. She wants to live in a world where this can exist. She can't give in. In fact, deep within her a switch is flipped, and nothing matters but the light. The light of her vision. The light from everywhere illuminating the room inside the house. The yard where Adam sits with Dad, the light. The light! The light!

"Maya?" Dharma startles her away from her one-thousand-mile stare. "Are you alright?"

"I am," Maya answers. She holds her arm out, noticing she's glowing with a radiating yellow light.

Dharma holds her hand and watches as the light spreads up her own arm and through her body. She reaches out and spreads it to Ubuntu, who throws her arms on Adam. He blooms in confidence again and reaches out to Nicu, spreading, slowly spreading this subtle glow. It comes from Maya's mind into reality. The riders glow and rise up from their retreat. From behind the mountainside they ride, emergent once again, and take it to the forces of the Dark Boards.

Even Tjikko rose from his slumber, as if he had heard a sweet tune float over the hills. He sat up and brushed the dust off his shoulders, and then went directly for Radu, to finish what he started.

The entire tri-fold army was renewed by Maya's spirit. The warriors of the Tree of Life lent to one another, second and third boards, to stack and multiply accordingly in their power of attack. While the lenders themselves assumed their animal forms, of gorillas, lions, panthers and certain of them elephants. This proved to be the most effective tactic of ground combat thus far.

The elves began unleashing attacks of air. Pneumatic darts from beneath their boards as vortex torpedoes spiraled into the soldiers, setting them back, some of them stunned, but the majority shaking it off, returning to combat one by one.

"It's not enough!" Bella yelled out.

Tjikko laid into Radu again leading with a shoving of his hardwood board directly into Radu's gut, knocking the wind out of him. Dropping the gloves, he simply began to wail on

Radu's face with his bare hands. This also proved to be a surprisingly effective tactic.

"You old—" Tjikko said and punched. "Saggy—" Punch again. "Plastic—" Hard punch. "Bag!" Tjikko said, knocking Radu back.

But Radu returned a board-kick to the side of Tjikko's knee, and when he bent down, a board kick uppercut to Tjikko's chin. Tjikko hunched again.

"Our first order will be to cover the forests with concrete." Radu said. "Get rid of the wretched mold of green."

Tjikko roared! He sent a missile, of his board, at Radu's head, but Radu dodged it. The board went sailing into the distance, and Radu continued his siege on Tjikko.

Dharma and Ubuntu stole glances of the barrage of their brother, but were unable to break from their own battles to help him. They tirelessly fended off Dracul and Arthur, and the other hoods, while simultaneously throwing everything they had, at the advancing legions of the Dark Boards.

But the soldiers of tungsten and mercury and dolomite just kept coming, winding into the distance. They trampled over riders of the Boardsmen, as they came. Slowly but surely the weight of the Dark Boards pushed south. The battle was pushed down through mountainous terrain, into a broad forest of towering pines.

The silky bright grey clouds of overcast afternoon, stretched across the landscape. Blended timeless grays, stretching thin, still stretching thin. They entered the pines.

Chapter 55

The forest was deep. The trees were spread evenly from eons of agreements. The undergrowth was a mossy all-covering blanket, crawling over downed logs and rocks. The pine forest was an open, living breathing battle ground. The gray sky permeated the space between the trees, giving green boughs and grey brown trunks, the shine and sheer of a white hard light. In this forest the cold wind was put to rest. All was still.

The Tungsten Soldiers entered. The Boardsmen gathered the troops once more among the trees to mount a final stand. Tjikko addressed them.

"Beyond the southern boundary of this forest lay the clearing within which Old Tjikko stands. If we don't stop them here..." Tjikko said.

"Out of the question," Dharma said.

The Dark Boards advanced through rows of trees. Their faces were as placid as their metallic make up. They could not be stopped.

"Any ideas?" Tjikko asked.

"Nope," Ubuntu said. "Oh— wait, how about we whoop those ugly metal tinmen. One of them messed my shoulder up." She said rotating her arm.

"I think that's the best idea," Maya said. "I vote for Ubuntu's plan."

"As a result of Maya's spirit, we have removed a good chunk of the army," Dharma said. "But we have not slowed their advance. We must push back!"

"It's like stopping gravity," Adam said.

"Aye, my pessimistic friend, aye," Tjikko said, looking at the raging battle.

Men were falling. Elves were falling. Good men fell. Good elves fell. Radu reigned supreme and floated boastfully through the forest with eight black hoods behind him. Tjikko contemplated Radu.

"They're nothing without Radu— and a handful of the other hooded generals," Tjikko said. "Without Radu, who will enact their final phase? Those oversized paper weights may not even make it through the door of Old Tjikko. She's a tricky tree. A picky tree. You need a soul, I know that."

"So, if we take the generals down, the soldiers run into the sea like some chicken with their heads cut off?" Adam asked.

"Exactly Adam, exactly," Tjikko said.

"Kazzo! Numo!" Ubuntu whistled.

"Right, —Windemere and Bella! Assemble!" Tjikko called.

The four riders came out from cover. Together they were nine good riders. Tjikko huddled up the group.

"I will take Radu—" Tjikko started.

"Will you, Tjikko?" Dharma interrupted. "Or do you need big sis to clean up your mess again?"

"I got him, Dharma," Tjikko assured her. "What? I got him right where I want him."

"Okay, but if I see you throwing punches ten feet in the ground again. I'm gonna come show him how a real rider does it."

"That's right," Ubuntu added.

"Sisters," Tjikko said, rolling his eyes, looking to Adam. "Now I remember why we don't visit much."

"Oh Tjikko, just looking out," Dharma said. She leaned over to him and messed up his already messy hair. "Go ahead. You got him."

"Okay," Tjikko said, regaining himself. "Now, me— I'll take Radu. Dharma," turning to her, "you take Arthur. Ubuntu you take Dracul. Adam and Maya, you take Argon."

Tjikko pointed.

"Windermere and Bella— you take Kala, the cave sister. She is fierce, but you can take her together. Kazzo and Numo— you take Syztra the Bold. When we all finish there will remain a few more hoods, but by that time, they too will have their tails between their legs. We will turn them around together. Plus, the last three bottom feeders know about as much as the rest of these lead brains!"

Tjikko rose.

"Ready?" Tjikko said.

"Ready," Adam said.

The others nodded heavily.

"Then let's crush these jokers!" Tjikko answered.

They turned out from behind the trees and led the charge. Tzara flew by on his board.

"Why did you just huddle?" He asked as he passed by. "What's the plan?"

"You take the birds!" Tjikko said. "We're going after the leaders!"

"Good plan!" Tzara said as he flew away. "I hunt these birds for sport! I will eat these birds for breakfast!"

The rest of the riders of elves and warriors had taken to weaving through the scattered and staggered trees. They were pinking the tin heads back and forth until they broke off, or spun over, or at least the soldier fell still to the ground.

The elves began to control the trees, bending the trunks with tricks of nature. They lured soldiers into gaps and whacked them with the trunks as they passed at high speeds. The metal soldiers met their match with living solid wood, deeply rooted in the earth.

Tjikko hovered up to Radu once more with thrice renewed determination.

"More, you say?" Radu asked. "You should just have a seat over there and wait for the concrete to pour. Get it? Instead of champagne we pour— oh forget it."

Radu swung up and around on his board, thrusting himself in a bizarre position, and initiated more board to board combat. They twisted and wrestled, throwing blows at each other. They went through the trees while weaving, stunning, recovering, punching, launching dark energy, and blasting back green energy light.

"You are the demon that deceives without reason!" Tjikko said.

"Whoa, whoa, whoa!" Radu responded. "You're mistaken! I do no deceiving!" Radu said, feigning hurt feelings.

"You have gone too far!" Tjikko said.

"We have not yet begun!" Radu said. "Join me!"

"I'd rather die!" Tjikko said back.

"I wish you would!" Radu snarled.

In the distance, Dharma and Arthur traded blows between the trees. Arthur sent his stone board spinning and whirring with glowing hot red light. Dharma dodged it acrobatically and sent a nose jab which emitted little golden arcs toward Arthur. Arthur dodged her attack with ease.

"You show much improvement from our meeting in the cave." Dharma offered.

"Thank you for noticing!" Arthur said, as he wove through the trees and throwing one big roundhouse kick.

"Why don't put your hood back on, Arthur?" Dharma said. "You look foolish." Dharma dodged and caught him with a board hook to the rib.

"Why don't you worry about your own wardrobe!" Arthur answered. He landed back a whip of big red-light energy, knocking Dharma to the earth.

Argon was no match for the twin attacks of Maya and Adam. They assaulted him from all angles, and with such speed, with such communicative coordinated cuts that his head was spinning. Then they cut him down.

"Alright!" Adam said.

"One down!" Maya said.

And they moved on to the remaining nameless hoods. The elves and warriors were getting thin. The puppets dwindled in their numbers. The fight raged on. A tangled mess of weaving through the trees.

"This better work!" Adam said, swerving after Maya.

Ubuntu took it to Dracul on the far side of the glen.

"I've been assigned to you— unfortunately!" Ubuntu said, beating back Dracul's face.

"The only one unfortunate is you!" Dracul retorted, with a flailing wild attack.

Ubuntu dodged and roundhouse whipped her board into Dracul's back, slashing him with his momentum into the ground.

"What was that about misfortune?" Ubuntu asked.

"Well... that is...that, fortune favors— the Dark Boards!" Dracul screamed and flipped up a rock and sent it flying at Ubuntu— with force.

The rock hit Ubuntu in the gut.

"You two-timing— low life— ugly—" Ubuntu mustered.

To the west Kala strikes down Windemere. He lays motionless in the dirt.

"Windermere!" Bella screamed. Her scream echoed through the trees. Tjikko takes his eye off Radu momentarily to see that good Windemere had fallen. Radu lost not a moment in slapping Tjikko in the back of his head. A devastating blow.

Ubuntu beats Dracul deep into the earth and buried him with dirt. She then rushes to the aid of Bella facing imminent defeat in Kala's rage of momentum after striking down Windemere. She hovers slowly, advancing over Bella. Ubuntu descends between them.

"That will do, Kala." Ubuntu utters gravely.

Dharma handles Arthur but she can't quite kill him. Tjikko gets beat up again like an old dog. Maya-Adam fly among the trunks of pine trees, tracking down the remaining generals. Through the trees they see Syztra. Suddenly she deals a crushing blow to Kazzo. He falls motionless to the ground, lying face up, eyes open in an infinite stare.

Jatta hears the wailing of his father and makes eye contact with Nicu, fighting his heart out. The two sons rush to their father.

"Father! No!" Nicu cries.

Jatta attempts to tend to his injuries, frantically looking for a way to prevent the end from coming.

"This is not the end," Kazzo says. "We will hug again. We will ride the green hills together like our dreams from here to paradise."

"Papa," Jatta mutters, whispers.

Jatta looks into his father's eyes. Nicu on the other side. They hold him as he drifts away.

Numo was facing Syztra on his own now. Jatta flew at him with rage, while Nicu stayed at Kazzo's side. But the Dark Soldiers pressed in his direction. Nicu fought them with a shattered heart, tears stream down his lost face.

The legions barely broke formation now. The efforts of the Boardsmen and the riders fading once again. Marching echoes through the forest. The Metal Army pushes down, squeezing Tjikko and his forces, out of the fray, out of the forest, into the clearing. In the distance Old Tjikko quivers in the wind.

Maya looks again, again at devastation. Adam couldn't take his stare away from Nicu's tears. The nightmare presses onward. The sea of metal caving in.

"They're just *too* heavy!" Adam said, faltering once more.

"Adam please! Will you just stop saying that?" Maya snaps. "They will be what you believe they are, and if you keep chanting that, then heavy they will be. Now, will you help me keep these cotton balls from reaching Old Tjikko?"

"Of course, Maya. I will fight till I lose sight." Adam said, with a daze-y look. "But those are some heavy cotton balls."

"—Adam! Ugh! They are *your* soul!" Maya said. "No wonder they're so dense!" Maya truly snapped, exasperated.

"Hey," Adam argued, half-heartedly.

"Your soul," Maya echoed to herself.

"I heard you," Adam replied.

"Adam," Maya started.

"I like your tone," Adam encouraged.

"We have to go back," Maya said, eyes opening.

"Wait— no— back where?" Adam asked, not wanting to know.

"The source," Maya said, turning to her brother.

"What source? No, no, no," he said while backing up.

"The tunnel, Adam," Maya said. "That is where this army gets its power from. They're nothing but solid metal. They have no motion without sorcery."

"I can't go back there Maya, I just..." Adam said, trailing off. "I can't."

"I need you, Adam!" Maya said, drawing near to him. "I know it's hard. But look!" She gestured to the tree line where the Dark Boards poured into the final valley now. "What choice do we have?"

Adam already couldn't look at all the heartache, the defeat. He couldn't look. He couldn't go. He couldn't do anything.

"Alright!" Adam said. "You're right. I can't let these demons take over our planet!"

And so, Maya and Adam searched for Dharma. They found her in the midst of battle, fighting Arthur.

"Mom!" Maya said.

Dharma gave what attention she could while fending Arthur off.

"Yes— Maya! What is it?" Dharma answered.

"The soldiers! the Dark Boards! They're getting their power from a source!" Maya said.

"Yes," Dharma said. "Yes. But—"

Dharma blasted Arthur back. He landed far, rolling, tumbling on the ground.

"The cave, mom! We have to cut it off! At the source!" Maya said.

"But the cave is— thousands of miles— days— we don't have time!" Dharma said.

Maya deflated.

"But, we don't have a choice!" Maya said desperately. "You know they will reach Old Tjikko."

Arthur rose again in the distance, slowly. Dharma stared vacantly in his direction. And then, with gravity, she looked to Maya.

"Where is Good Syv?" Dharma asked. "He can get you there. Take Syv, and go as fast as you possibly can. We will hold this army off until you return. Let me remind you that you only have one shot at this!"

Dharma stared into her daughter's eyes and then into her son's.

"I don't want to lose you again" she said.

"Then let us go," Maya said.

Dharma's eyes filled with tears. She redoubled her courage.

"Go baby," Dharma said, with boldness.

Maya hugged her mother. Adam hugged his mother. They took one last look at the impending doom. They hastened to Good Syv.

"Syv!" Maya said. Syv turned from tireless flying while swiping, fruitlessly whacking giant metal heads. He stared at Maya as she spoke: "—we need a ride!"

Chapter 56

Syv descended with a gust of wind amidst a clearing in the overcast silver forest. Maya hopped off her board before it could fully land. Adam followed closely after her. Syv came to a stop, and joined Maya and Adam with their boards under their arms.

Through the long grass, they approached the semi-megalithic stones. Between the pines, at the foot of a steep cliff of dirt and rock, the pile of stones remained, with one dark shadow of a crevice, ominous and luring.

"Why, Maya?" Adam asked.

They stood at the mouth of the cave. They could feel the cold air expiring from the opening. Maya looked at Adam with a display of heightened senses. Together they looked back into the cave.

"Come on," Maya said.

Through the crack they moved, into darkness. Once inside, the three of them mounted their boards, and with their boards illuminated the caverns.

Bats flew out from the sub-crustaceous inner entrance. Syv flinched.

"Romania," Adam said to Syv.

The tunnel of the cave descended lower down into the bowels of the earth. They came to the zone of drooling pillars, forming cells and stepped shelves. The stalactites dripped and met stalagmites, thinning the middle, like the slobber in the corner of a vicious dog's mouth.

Down they went, with Maya leading them, through rolling waves of cells until they emerged into a high open space. Before them lay the jagged gulch, the decadent entrance of columns on the other side.

"Some inscription," Syv said, inspecting. "I speak Dark Boards. It says: In the shadow of the light we have our birth. In the darkness of eternity, we have our place."

The riders hovered near the edge of the dark chasm.

"Why, Maya?" Adam asked, slightly turning to her, with his head still stuck on the inscription.

Maya didn't answer. She led the way across the gulch. The light of three boards barely made a dent, in the unknown darkness of the pit. They crossed through the concrete gates into the lair. The city was empty, deeply silent, ringing.

"I heard about some guy who was lost in a cave for days," Adam said. "And when they found him, he was clicking two rocks together, to keep himself from going crazy from the silence."

They glided up the pathway to the field of slate. The flicker of the torches was the loudest thing around. They road across the open concrete surface. Adam's jest of denial faded from his face. He cringed at thoughts of Marcus, the brainwashing. Suddenly Adam fell to the floor. Memories flashed through his mind of hooded figures in the darkness, the white light of the flame, the concrete rooms— everywhere. The way they talked, the signals they reacted to like systematic mind, like schools of fish, the stimulus of fear.

"Adam!" Maya turned.

Syv and Maya rushed to help him up.

"I'm okay," Adam said.

Sitting there, they heard a sound. The sound was faint but slightly louder than the flickering light. It was coming from beyond the line of temples. They shared a look, that they all had heard the sound. They hovered over to the edge where their boards could illuminate the areas where no torches had been placed.

There, below the city, was the village of the gray and tattered creatures. They were still there, wandering, working. Some were pushing wheel barrows full of gray sand like ashes.

"They are the indigenous people of the cave." Adam said. He lifted up his board illuminating slums which stretched back deep and faded into darkness. "Or indigenous of *something*," he added.

Maya looked in disbelief at the hordes of scattered people wandering through the streets.

"Come on," Maya said, as she turned. "Let's get this done and get out of here."

They got back to the level of the slate, the temples, the upper class. They crossed the slate and came to the top of the extremely wide descending staircase, past the podium where Adam had his soul ripped out, and down into the pitch-black void. A second mouth inside, lying in wait at the end of the cave.

An even colder air expired from this massive hole that opened in the great cave wall. Cold air and something else— A thread of high pitch sound, like a string flowing slowly in a stream.

Adam looked at Maya for a while. Maya looked into the blackness of the tunnel. She turned to Adam.

"Why?" Adam said once more. And he sat down on the top step.

"It was no accident," Maya said. "Meeting Zeddefungo, getting lost."

Adam looked up at Maya.

"We were called to do this," Maya said.

"Called by who Maya?" Adam replied. "Right now, the only thing calling us is some demon woman in the black hole."

Maya stood for moment.

"I can't do it alone, Adam," she said, reaching out her hand.

"Take Syv," Adam said.

Maya put her head down. Adam looked into the tunnel. He looked down at the ground between his feet. He turned and looked over his shoulder at the City of the Dark Boards, the high pantheon, the lower temples. Then he looked up again at Maya.

"I can't let any of this happen to another soul," Adam said. "—Let's extract that root!"

***

At Tjikko, the steel soldiers advanced across the broad and shallow valley. Tjikko, exhausted, gave it everything he had against Radu. He threw a board attack, but it was thwarted by Radu.

"Give up, Tjikko!" Radu commanded. "Take a look around. It's over."

"We don't do that— giving up thing," Tjikko said, breathing heavily.

Radu rolled his eyes. "Fine, fine, I always offer —save myself some trouble you know."

And the fight continued. Ubuntu aided Bella and the others in the termination of the final few Dark Board generals.

"Come on! Come on!" Ubuntu called out fiercely as they finished off Kala. "Numo, Bella! We have to hold the soldiers. Cover me!"

Ubuntu sped toward the forces, she jumped into a front flip, landing and releasing a blow of energy, a wave that leveled the two first rows of soldiers. Wiping the sweat from her brow she continued to attack.

Dharma witnessed her heroism. She turned to Arthur with her board of glowing flames.

"This ends now!" Dharma exclaimed.

"You're right about that," Arthur said. "The mighty Dharma," He said with a smirk. "I thought she'd be mightier!"

Arthur attacked, but Dharma dodged him with ease. She turned and fired on him, blowing him across the field into the dirt.

"I said— this ends— now." Dharma's board began to charge and hum with light.

"Wait! Wait!" Arthur said, cringing and taking off his hood. "I'm just a cave dweller. Drafted by the Dark Boards against my will! Brainwashed— like your son! Right?!" he smiled madly.

The hum of Dharma's board decreased slightly.

"I... I... Wanted to help him," Arthur said. "Really I did. I was planning on it." Arthur spoke to Dharma softening in the air. Suddenly he rolled backwards popping up onto his board. "But it only took him days to lose what took them years to do to me!" he said quickly before he powered up his board with red light and tried to fire off shot.

Dharma beamed a yellow laser larger than Arthur's body that roasted him into the ground where he stood. "Shut up, Art," she said.

Just then Radu sent Tjikko blasting through the air again. Dharma rushed and caught him before he hit the dirt. He was tattered, burnt and bleeding. "How about some help brother?" Dharma offered.

Ubuntu slung attacks left and right into the metal army.

"Ubuntu!" Dharma shouted across the field. "Let's waste this ugly hood!"

Ubuntu sped across the field. "Next time let us take the leader! Just for future reference, you know. Because, clearly..." she said.

"I get it!" Tjikko growled.

"That's my brother!" Ubuntu laughed.

Tjikko launched the attack. A vicious Flying V of three enclosed on Radu. They shot beams and bands and boards at Radu, who dipped and ducked and dodged them all.

"So limber for such an old— old man," Ubuntu said.

"Let me teach you kids a lesson," Radu said. He emitted a slicing beam from each end of his board, and began to rotate with momentum, knocking them all back, flipping through the air.

***

Maya and Adam entered the wide mouth of the great tunnel, followed cautiously by Syv into the belly of the beast. The supersonic ringing, floating passed them through the air. Illuminated by the boards, the tunnel walls appeared to be ribbed and brown.

"What are we supposed to do when we get down there?" Adam asked Maya. "Just pull the plug? We don't even know what could be waiting for us," Adam said.

"We must be ready for anything, at any time," Maya said. "Don't worry yet."

Up ahead of them, something was appearing. Everyone prepared. Maya peered ahead at the figure. Out of the darkness appeared a gray cave dwelling man in a tattered robe. Wandering aimlessly out of the tunnel, he took no notice of the riders.

Adam looked at Maya. They continued. Soon they came to a point in the tunnel where shallow water started. First with puddles, then a uniform sliver of depth coated the cave floor.

"What the heck is this?" Adam asked, looking at the water.

As they went further the water got deeper. Another cave dweller waded through the water, sloshing. Soon another. The riders really began to wonder what was going on. Soon the water rose so high it was half way up the massive tunnel wall. The riders skimmed the surface and proceeded. They proceed until the water rose to such a level that they had to crouch to enter any further.

"Sooo... That's it?" Adam asked. "No root? No source?"

"The source is down there," Maya said. "There's gotta be a way to keep going."

They stood up.

"The boards!" Syv said.

Maya looked.

"We can dive the waters," Syv said. "Keep your feet on the boards and they will give you breath. If you need to speak. Direct your thoughts to me. I will hear you. I will translate between us."

Maya looked at Adam.

"After you," Adam said.

Maya tucked under the water. She crouched and submerged on her board beneath the tunnel ceiling. Soon the three of them were gliding underwater. The three boards illuminated the subaqueous cavern. Adam looked at Maya with wide excited eyes, if only for a moment. They floated further down the tunnel, down.

Suddenly the tunnel emptied out from the bottom of a large rock wall. They had been let out into an entirely open underwater world, but there was nothing for the eye to see. No bounds. No walls, no ground, no light. Just this flat rock out of which they came.

Maya looked at Adam once again. Adam looked at Syv.

"He says: Now what?" Syv said to Maya.

Maya looked at Adam with dull expression. Then she looked around. Nothing. She floated lower, down away from the rock, and soon some features deep below them began to come into view. Rocks, cliffs, something. She motioned for the others to follow.

As they floated, the light of board emitting pie shaped beams into the depths, the features became clearer. They approach the objects and realize they are looking at the ruins of an ancient under water city. Adam and Maya look, with shock, to the ruins in their midst. The three riders float through the rows of buildings that, all crestfallen and destroyed, black algae that creeping up the forms.

Maya looked at Syv.

"She says: Be on your guard," Syv said to Adam.

Cautiously they explore the ruins, waiting for some leviathan to emerge, considering if they should have brought backup. Suddenly, Adam sees something. Another of the tattered cave dwellers— walking on the sea floor, and paddling with its hands. Adam signals Maya and Syv. They watch as the creature approaches a massive gulch at the city limits. Adam looks at Maya, wide-eyed.

The creature finds a ledge into the trench and descends. Maya starts to follow. Adam shakes his head.

They pass over the ledge of the trench to find, there at the bottom, swaths of cave dwelling men wandering, huddling, bumping into each other.

Maya approaches the numbers. At the bottom of the gulch, in the center, seems to be a dense gathering of the gray creatures. At the center of the group, an inflammation of men is covering something. They claw and scratch at the mass.

Maya and Adam descend to the gulch at ocean floor. They pass between the outlying creatures of the huddle. Their hair is black, thinning, sparse. Their skin is gray and blotchy, approaching translucence. Their teeth black and sharp. Their noses flat. Their eyes black, or closed. They claw at some undulating black mass, some mound, branching, clutching the ground, breathing.

Adam looks at faces as he passes. He waves and snaps his fingers to get their attention. Nothing. Maya approaches the black mass. Subtle white, red electricity flows below the black translucent tar. The creatures scratch and claw the surface, push each other out of the way.

Adam passes by one man. Suddenly he double-takes. He returns to the man and examines him. His heart begins to pulse, to throb. He stares with wild disbelief at what he sees.

"Zeddefungo?" he says out loud, emitting bubbles in the water. "Zeddefungo!" he said. He begins to scream and shake the man.

Maya turns, confused. She goes to Adam. There she finds him shaking this old cave creature. Screaming something.

Adam turns to Maya. Frantically he tries to call to her attention. "Zeddefungo!" he shouts.

Bubbles. Maya turns to Syv.

"Did he say Zeddefungo?" Maya asks.

Syv confirms.

Maya looks incredulously at this man that Adam's shaking. Suddenly she sees— that he is right. But this doesn't make her any less confused. She looks at Adam. Her heart drops to the bottom of her stomach. Before her stands her brother. His face has begun to become gray. His hair begins turning black, strands falling to the dust. Maya turns in horror to Syv, only to find that it is happening to Syv too.

Maya shakes Adam and tries to tell him. Adam is panicking. Maya is panicking. She pulls black hairs from Adam's head and holds them to his face. Adam is petrified with freight. He sees that Maya is turning gray. He sees that Syv is turning gray. Maya stares into the underwater dust, wide eyed, and contemplating. Adam turns to fly, to leave— she grabs his hand. Adam looks with deeply furrowed brow at Maya's arm pulling him.

Maya looks at Syv.

"I know what we have to do," Syv says for Maya to Adam.

Adam maintains his facial expression, shakes his head "No".

"We have to destroy whatever that thing is over there. That thing everybody's scratching at."

Adam looks to Syv.

"How do you suggest we do that?" Syv translates to Maya.

Maya looks to the reverberating mass. Slowly she approaches. Adam grabs hold of Zeddefungo. He and Syv follow Maya to the epicenter.

Maya faces on her board the mass. Focusing, she tries to summon what she learned from Dharma in the forest. How to enter deep into herself. Into her soul, the soul of rider, where the form of her board resides.

Her board begins to glow. Adam looks at Syv. Soon is her entire body glowing purple. Cave creatures quit their scratching, back away. Maya centers, focuses deep. Thinks of laser beam of purple light. Destroy the source. Remove the Dark Boards from existence. And with one final push she screams in bubbles, giving everything she's got. But. one final orb emerges. Purple, floating from her board nose. Floating, the bubble spirals in the water blowing. Maya hangs her head. Searches her mind, begins to try again, but doubt is flooding. This is failure. Maya breaks.

Adam shakes her shoulder, his face completely grey. He points. Maya looks up. The orb is floating toward the dark mass, radiating in the water, it's spiraling stops, it hovers true, in radiation growing. Soon the purple bubble comes in contact with the sickness, source of darkness stretching through the canyon, crawling up the walls. A crack of brilliant luminous purple, another crack, splitting spreading through the dark, brilliant purple beams forth from the cracks and turns the black reverberations to a frozen purple-white. The mass explodes into thousands of shards of purple light.

A hole beneath the mass is revealed. A hole in ocean floor. Maya, the cave dwellers, Adam, Syv, and Zeddefungo are pulled towards and through the hole. With water they are pushed into the orifice. Water's pouring through but isn't rushing— floating. In the blackness of the void they enter. Floating, through the darkness, spinning, boards illuminating. Maya gray, Syv and Adam gray and all completely empty cave dwellers floating through the void.

***

In the Valley at Old Tjikko's feet, Jatta fought valiantly among the ranks of metal soldiers. By now they had passed the halfway mark of this final clearing. Jatta sent a drilling kick flip towards one of the soldiers. To Jatta's surprise, it took the soldiers forearm clear off his body. The soldier slightly surprised too, looked down at his arm. Jatta caught his board returning, and through a backside upper cut, spinning into the chin of the soldier. His head broke clean off his neck. Slightly confused, Jatta inspected the soldier in passing. He noticed something on the soldier's body— RUST. The soldiers had begun to corrode. All around, Jatta looked as brown, orange, green corrosion crept over the Army of Soldiers, one by one.

"The soldiers!" Jatta shouted. "The soldiers are rusting!"

Nicu looked around and saw that Jatta was right. Somehow, the soldiers were becoming covered in rust. Nicu and Bella looked at each other. They turned and attacked. For once, the soldiers took damage from the attacks of the riders.

Jatta looked around.

"Attack with everything!" Jatta screamed. "They are weak! Attack!"

The birds in the sky began to short circuit and fly 'neath heavy load. The puppets took advantage, dropping one bird, now another.

The elves, the warriors of the Tree of Life and the puppets, all around began, for the first time in this battle, to push back.

Rays of the evening sun began to pour out from the clouds, and soon the sun came into a clearing in the open sky.

The rusty soldiers crunched and stiffened, but they were no push-overs, they returned the efforts of the riders and continued slowly to advance, followed by another push back from the riders.

"We're moving them!" Jatta cried. "We've got to push! Come on! Everything you've got!"

There came an intense stalemate. Nobody was moving anywhere. Many were being slain.

***

Maya in the void, her last remaining consciousness, before becoming permanently gray, she sees a light. A twinkling little, white light. She straightens her spinning. She looks back at Adam and the others. Holding on this, focus on this little light with all awareness of her being she brings it to herself, or she brings herself to the light. Adam in his final freedom follows Maya, dragging Zeddefungo, dragging others.

Soon the crew of riders crosses the void. The line of riders extending back into the water, to the hole in ocean floor, floating from the hole in anti-gravity, through the sea of anti-anything.

Approaching the twinkling light, Maya notices another one, there, more. Soon she floats among a sea of little diamond lights. She holds her hands up feeling warmth. She sees the pigment start returning to her hands. She looks at Adam coming fast and gaining hair and color in his face, amazed.

"Maya!" Adam shouts. "They're stars!"

They look with revelation and amazement at each other. Maya looks back at the other cave dwellers. They all return to color slowly, looking at their arms and legs confused, riders reaching out and grabbing, hugging on each other. Finally, boards are produced beneath their feet.

"Who are these people?" Maya says to Adam.

Zeddefungo floats up on his board by Maya and Adam.

"These are angel riders Maya!" Zeddefungo shouted. "You have done the impossible. You have restored us from eternal toil. You did it, Maya! You did it!"

The crowd of riders floated through the stars.

"These can't be stars!" said Maya.

"They look like stars," Adam said, spinning through space.

"They are stars," Zeddefungo said. "But the question is— what is that?" He pointed to what appeared to be a big fat white star ahead. Just a giant circle. A flat white light among the stars.

***

Radu looked back in confusion.

"What are you doing!?" He spewed with slobber to his soldiers. "No matter! I will just have to do this on my own!"

He glowed with red and white flames in his entire aura. An energy black smoke surrounded him. He started rapid firing automatic missiles in all directions. Heat seeking doomsday devices, knocking Tjikko, Dharma, Ubuntu down onto their backs and out of service, dropping riders left and right among the crowd.

"I have come too far!" Radu cried madly.

Jatta, Nicu, Bella dodged the missiles; and saw Radu approaching rapidly the tree.

"Nicu! Bella! —Radu!!" Jatta yelled.

They blasted off in his direction. They came upon a fiery Radu, and launched an attack, as a last effort to save the tree.

Radu exploded waves of grey clear power knocking them all back. They lay eyes closed, aside. Then, Tjikko picked himself up once more, and lunged at Radu who was closing in on the tree.

"NO!!" Radu screamed with force. His voice was full of charged darkness. "This is— over!"

From Radu's being came a black-dark power, like a snake, and drove Tjikko into the ground. From there Tjikko looked on, unable to move, as Radu sped towards the tree. The sun was hanging low below the clouds.

***

Maya floated towards the giant, flat white circle in the stars with curiosity.

"That's a big star." Adam said.

The entire crowd extending in a caravan of people through the stars were led by Maya coming up to this big star. And as they approached, it grew.

Maya went faster and faster.

"Well don't run into it!" Adam yelled. "It's probably hotter than heck!"

"Pull back!" Zeddefungo yelled.

"I can't! I'm not going toward it anymore!" Maya cried. "I'm being pulled!"

***

Tjikko stared up into the sky at Radu, floating before Old Tjikko, white cloak flapping in the wind.

"You lose!!" Radu screamed madly. "This is it! This is the end!" Radu turned 'round. The clouds had pulled back like a hood revealing evening sun and deep blue skies. "Take a good look. This will be the last blue sky the world will ever know."

Tjikko hung his head. Dharma and Ubuntu, stared up unable to move.

"Viva la Dark Boards!!" Radu yelled madly.

He blasted off at Old Tjikko, only 30 feet away and closing the gap fast. With festering smile, he started cracking up while speeding toward the tree, to claim the world for evil. But just as he reached the tree he was stopped in his tracks, smacking flat and falling back on his back in the rock and grass. He held his damaged face and looked up at the tree in utter confusion.

A wall of puppets manifested from invisibility, standing linked like chain, three puppets thick.

"Not today!" Tzara cried.

"Puppet wall!!" Ignatz screamed, raving.

Radu levitated to the top level of the tree. Only wooden beings stood between Radu and utter success.

"Move," Radu said, "or I'll turn you into firewood."

The sun had dropped directly behind the peak of Old Tjikko.

"Absolutely not," Tzara said.

"Suit yourself," Radu said.

***

"Brace yourselves!" Maya cried. "We're coming in faaaast!"

They careened through the glowing disk, streaming into the portal of light, and out into a sunny mountain day.

***

And pouring forth from the sun at Old Tjikko's peak like class five rapids were the fallen Hero riders of all time. Radiant, colorful, glorious. Led at the helm by Maya and Adam, followed by Syv and Zeddefungo. They barreled through Radu like a stampede and they didn't stop there. They barreled through the entirety of the Dark Boards Army. Like a freight train snake of massacres slashing the corroded soldiers that remained to bite sized bits, leaving no trace.

The rest of the riders— the puppets, the jungles, the elves— laid down their heavy loads, and turned to join the wave of mutilation[1]. Tjikko, Dharma, and Ubuntu sat up in pure joyous disbelief. Renewed with strength, they took to the sky, only to have to do nothing but to sit back and watch the carnage of the parade of destruction. The puppets cheered and threw their hats. They buzzed around with joy and jubilation.

"Now that's what I call imp-impeccable timing," Ignatz stuttered.

Ubuntu put her arm on Dharma's shoulder as they watched the win. "Your baby did it!" Ubuntu said.

"*Our* baby," Dharma said.

Maya lead the dragon train around, beaming with joy. Bright smile on her face. Wind in her hair. The sun was shining down upon her. They had won. They had defeated the Dark Boards.

Adam came to Maya in the air and hugged her spinning on their boards.

"You did it, sis, you really did it!" Adam exclaimed.

"We did it Adam! Are you crazy?" Maya answered. "Without you I would give up every day."

"What are you talking about? All I do is doubt, and sit down!" Adam said.

"Someone's gotta do that for the two of us," Maya said. "Without you I'd actually have to think about how scary it all is."

"Thank you?" Adam said. "I mean— you're welcome?"

"I don't know," Maya hugged him, smiling.

Tjikko came to Radu lying in the dirt and rock before Old Tjikko. Ubuntu and Dharma joined him, encircling the fallen leader. Radu was starting to prop himself up, but then fell beneath the weight of his defeat and his injuries. He cast up a hideous, vengeful look at the three great riders. "What are you going to do?" he snarled. "Kill me?"

"Yes!" Ubuntu answered.

"No," Dharma said, glancing at Ubuntu.

"No?" Ubuntu asked.

"We're going to give you what you need." Dharma said.

"The universe?" Radu asked with condescension in his voice.

"What you need!" Dharma said. "Not what you think you want," She rounded him and came closer.

"What you need— is a nap," Dharma said.

Tjikko looked at Ubuntu, confused.

"A nap?" Radu said rudely. "What the heck are you talking about— a nap?"

"I'm talking about— give it a rest— Radu," Dharma said.

Radu pondered for a moment. "Oh yes, lovely, a nap is what I need," he said. "And I'll never, ever dream of harming anyone again."

"No... you won't," Dharma said. She stepped back and held out her board, up and down, at arm's length in front of her face. Her board began to power glowing yellow.

Ubuntu did the same and held her board in front of her. Her board began to glow a deep Ubuntu-orange. Tjikko held his board up glowing forest green.

"What kind of nap is this?" Radu said, panic coming over his face.

"A deep one," Ubuntu said.

"Next-level nap," said Dharma, smiling.

Dharma, Ubuntu and Tjikko encircled Radu. There boards reached full charge and discharge three immaculate proton supersonic beams. The orange, green, and yellow light triangulated his position.

"What kind of nap is thiiis!?" Radu asked again, screaming.

From rider to rider emanated a whirring, racing circle of the green, yellow, and orange light.

"Mind if I join you?" Zeddefungo asked as he dismounted from the sky.

"Welcome back brother," Dharma said.

Zeddefungo joined the quaternary, holding up his board, glowing royal blue.

"What kind of nap is thiiiiiis!?" Radu echoed, caving in from proton beams.

—Boot—

He imploded and disintegrated. Black smoke and sugar emanated from his old location.

"A long one," Zeddefungo finished, eyebrows up.

The Four Boardsmen came together in the center of the circle, pressing heads on one another.

"Zefu," Tjikko said. "I can't express how good it is to see you again."

They hugged each other tight, closing eyes.

<u>Act VII</u>

Chapter 57

Adam and Maya are coming in for a landing. The sun is tangerine and big, hanging low in the sky. It pours warm light into the fjord where riders gather on the terrace, at the water's edge.

The Four Boardsmen are standing in a circle amongst the crowd, conversing among themselves and sharing the joy, the pleasure, the relief, the accomplishment of victory with anyone who approaches them or celebrates in passing. The entire fjord— the terrace, the walkways, the sky— is full of champion energy— darting around hugging each other, tears of joy, hand signals of reenactments of valor that will be passed down for generations.

Adam hops off his board and tucks it under his arm, making a B line for the Boardsmen. Maya gracefully descends behind him. She picks up her board and walks slowly after Adam. She closes her eyes and breathes in deep, release, she lets go of everything and fills with this beautiful moment.

Adam rushes up to Zeddefungo and surprises him with a giant hug.

"Zeddefungo!" Adam shouts right into Zeddefungo's body. "It's really you."

Maya strolls up to the group.

"I missed you too Adam," Zeddefungo says, hugging back as soon as he realizes what's going on.

"The dynamic duo," Ubuntu says, as she smiles at Adam and Maya.

Dharma hugged her daughter, then her son.

"You have both acted with the finest of honor, and the keenest of intuition. And now, as a result, not only has the head of the Dark Boards been severed, but so too has the root."

"Uygh!" Zeddefungo said, cringing. "No need to utter such utterances anymore." He began to dance and sing a merry tune. "Ding dong, the witch is dead, the wicked witch is dead[2]!"

"What witch?" Tjikko asked, looking dumb.

"Yo mama, that's who!" Zeddefungo answered.

A few of the riders, back from the grave, came up to Zeddefungo.

"Zeddefungo, Dharma, Ubuntu, Tjikko," they said, looking around and embracing everyone. "It has been too long."

"It has been too impossible!" Tjikko said.

"That too," the riders said. "There's that. But now, thanks to Maya—"

"How do you know my name?" Maya said.

The riders gave a knowing smile and continued, "—we have returned,"

"Hey! I helped," Adam added.

Maya put her arm around her brother. He looked at her with mock indignity.

"What are you guys going to do now?" Maya asked, looking around at all the flock of resurrected riders— slightly luminous, mixing with the crowds.

"We will be here," the riders shrugged. "The world is bigger than you know."

"And older too," Adam said, rolling his eyes.

"Yes," the riders said, confused at Adam's tone. "The two are not so unrelated."

"Zeddefungo?" Adam swiveled rudely. "What is this, your third life then?"

"Uh, that *I* know of, yes," Zeddefungo said. "Like your mother, I remember somewhat of something of a past life," Zeddefungo said, as he looked up and away. "Like tweed. I remember lots of tweed."

Adam shook his head as if his hair was wet, then he squinted.

"But unlike our mother, you have died again and— here you are again." Adam said, as he pried.

"Yes, what is this, a court trial?" Zeddefungo replied.

"Kind of," Adam answered. "I just— don't get it."

"You're a human, buddy," Zeddefungo said, as he patted Adam on the back. "Your life is full of details. Answers. Knowledge. All wrong by the way." Zeddefungo looked at Dharma. "I remember my first life. Anyway, this— what we've done here, what *you've* done here— has begun to put an end to it all. Definitively so. Nice work. Now the world will— unbeknownst to them— levitate, from the little weights once holding them down— also unbeknownst to them. Y'all know nothing. But I knew," Zeddefungo said, as he grabbed Maya and Adam by the shoulders. "I knew you had it in you. I didn't know how, but I'm telling you, I literally knew it— for a fact. Remember when I told you? And you were like, 'We're just kids!'" Zeddefungo said, as he stepped around in dramatic fashion, with his hands on his face dramatically.

"Well, we could ride the boards, so..." Maya said.

"Yes! There were hints!" Zeddefungo said.

"So when I die will I become a rider?" Adam asked.

"Well, I believe you— already are," Zeddefungo assured Adam.

"Am I on my third life or my second?" Adam asked seriously.

"There are no numbers my boy. You are an exception in the riders that's for sure. Some kind of first-life human detail world boy, with a heart of gold. Whose sister and himself have saved the universe!"

"And for that," Dharma said, "we owe you everything."

"And the people of this world will never understand the service you have done." Ubuntu said.

"That's not necessary guys," Maya said, lowering herself, lifting them up from bowing. "I'm just glad you're okay. We're okay. You know?" She looked around at joyous elves, laughing jungle warriors and proud puppets. "Look at all this."

They all dog piled on Maya in a giant group hug.

"You might be on your seventh life Maya," the resurrected riders said.

"I thought there were no numbers!" Adam said, looking back at Zeddefungo.

Jatta and Nicu approached from within the crowd beaming with joy and victory. They joined the pile in the giant group hug. Jatta found Maya and hugged her, lifting her up a little.

"I can't believe it, Maya!" Jatta said. "Hahaaa we have done it! Ubuntu we have done it! Praise the Great Spirit!"

"Ubuntu, these kids, " Tjikko said, "we've all got ourselves some— you know we just— you have all proven yourselves, worthy of anything. I am humbled by your bravery."

"Thank you Tjikko," Jatta said. Jatta paused and lowered his head.

"What is it Jatta?" Ubuntu asked.

"Does this mean," Jatta said, lifting his head, "that because Zeddefungo and the riders have returned— does this mean— other fallen riders— we may see them again?" he asked. His eyes were begging for the answer.

The group looked at each other.

"Your father is out there somewhere, Jatta," Zeddefungo stepped in. "Let these things take their course."

Jatta nodded, but put his head down.

"But I will be with you through this," Zeddefungo said, as he put his hand on Jatta's shoulder.

Tjikko put his hand on Jatta's shoulder. Together Ubuntu, Dharma, Maya, Adam, and Jatta, put their hands on Nicu's shoulders.

"This is only the beginning," Zeddefungo said. "Come! Let us rejoice in the certainty of this action that has been set into motion."

"I don't know what you just said Zefu, but I think it translates to: This calls for a feast!" Tjikko said. "Where did we leave off? I bet the cake is still fresh on the tables and the wine too. But don't eat the meat— oh don't eat the meat!" Tjikko said, as he trailed off toward the castle.

Just then Tzara came up, followed by Jaccapo, Ignatz and Anastasia. They were overwhelmed with joy and bouncing off the celebrating people like ping pong balls

"Whoooo is that?" Tzara came up tackling, swinging madly Adam to the ground. One by one they tackled Maya and piled onto Adam.

"Ooooh, you should have seen us Adam," Tzara said. "Did you see us? We were smashing evil smoke birds!"

"I saw you!" Adam exclaimed.

"No such luck with those metal fellas," Tzara confessed. "—Smashed my cousin to bits."

"Pinocchio?" Adam asked. "He'll be back though, right? Cuz you all regenerate or something, so he'll be back I think—"

"I don't know how it works for Puppets," Tzara said.

"Maya!" Jaccapo yelled. "Maya did you see us? Did you guys see us with the wall? You didn't see us. You guys were gone— ooh, we saved the day! Hooray! Okay, so we get our trophies now, or what?"

"The trophy is the salvation and renewal of the earth," Maya said.

"Horrible, I must have a statue built," Tzara said.

"Does this mean we're coming out of the basement?" Jaccapo asked.

"We're coming out of the basement," Tzara said. "We are coming out of the shadows."

"Oh, I love the sun," Ignatz said.

"We've got invisibility now, and respect— we should be given medals of honor— We need medals!" Tzara said. "Something that says: We are not sticks, we are wooden beings, do not throw us in the wood chipper on clean-up day—"

"Poor Chuck," Jaccapo said, head down. "No matter! The world is changing."

"Puppets rights! Puppets rights!" Ignatz chanted.

"You are always welcome to visit the Tree of Life," Ubuntu said.

"You mean it?" Anastasia said.

"Of course!" Ubuntu said. "You are heroes!"

"Oh, I've always wanted to see the majestic jungles of Africa." Anastasia said, beaming with joy.

"Thank you, thank you all," Tzara said. "One day, we're minding our business, fighting robots daily. Then this emo boy walked into Tinseltown and changed our lives forever. Aaah..." he sighed.

"And it's only just beginning," Adam said.

Anastasia looked at Adam. And Tzara caught them looking at each other with a twinkle in their eyes. Maya peered at this.

Bella entered the scene, sincerely. "Thank you, guys," she said to Maya and Adam. "I don't know what we would have done, what Old Tjikko would have done without you!"

"No Bella, thank *you*," Maya said, giving her a hug. "The kindness and spirit of your people has been a revelation. A refreshing festiveness."

"Thank you," Bella smiled. "Don't forget to visit— any time!"

Tjikko came out holding cakes. "Bella? ...Bella?" he said, as he searched the crowds for her.

"Right here, Tjikko," Bella answered, waving.

"Right," Tjikko said. "Bella, in light of good Windermere's...absence." Tjikko bowed. "You have become my right hand...elf...person."

"Woman, Tjikko. Right hand woman." Bella suggested.

"Right," Tjikko said. "Well, right hand woman, um, since we will have no foes to defend for some time to come, I will need some help with all these cakes."

"Dharma, Ubuntu," Tjikko addressed them. "Why don't you guys stay a while?"

"Oh, surely we will stay for dinner," Dharma said.

"No, I mean for a few days, a week, and a month. What have you got to do? The world will sleep safely and soundly," Tjikko said.

"Unbeknownst to them!" Zeddefungo said, yelling from the back of the group.

"You guys came up here, all— "Zeddefungo's dead! The Dark Boards are rapidly approaching with my lost son's soul as fuel!" We didn't even get a chance to hit the slopes. Let me show you guys the great white north." Tjikko said.

Dharma and Ubuntu shared a look, deciding.

"A few days wouldn't hurt," Dharma shrugged, looking at Ubuntu.

Adam and Maya became excited.

"Sure," Ubuntu said. "I can show you a thing or two about riding. Old Tjikko needs a sharpening."

"That's what I'm talking about!" Tjikko said. "We have feasts and beds for everyone! Elves, get this girl some help," he said with his arms on Bella's shoulders.

Bella smiled.

"You know what?" he said to Bella, taking pause. "I'll take care of this. You enjoy the feast, and I'll meet you there."

So, they feasted three nights. They saw the sights: The great white north and Northern Lights. They rode frozen rivers. They saw the North Pole. They were as free as could be. Tjikko said it was so. And they visited dwarves and North Pole cousins. They thought the story was over but it wasn't.

"Good bye Tjikko," Dharma said. "You know where to find us."

"Right," Tjikko said. "The Tree of Life and the mountain down behind us?"

Ubuntu looked at Dharma and they both looked at Tjikko.

"I think I'm going to stay with Ubuntu for a while," Dharma said. "I think I like people."

So, the Tree of Life group, and the puppets, got on the caravan. Their next stop was somewhere in over-there-land.

Chapter 58

They stood at the entrance of the old run-down theatre, where the puppets had begun to remodel.

"Good bye Maya... Good bye Adam," Tzara said.

"Aaaah!!" someone shrieked upon seeing a talking puppet. Then ran into a trash can upon seeing the puppet turn and wave to them.

"It sure is gonna be a different world," Adam said, watching the woman pick herself up from her fall.

"Yes," said Tzara with wooden stare.

A man with a cane stopped.

"I have a question." He said.

"Hold your question sir,"

"Um.. until when?"

"What?"

"......*What?*"

"What is your question, sir?" Tzara asked.

"What's going on?" he asked. "I mean, I have never seen a puppet—"

"Next question," Tzara said.

"But—"

"Sir I really don't know how it is that I walk and talk," Tzara said. "All I know," Tzara flicked him in the head, "is that it's real."

Adam stepped aside as the man with the cane walked away confused.

"I don't know," Maya looked at Adam with worry. "Are you guys going to be okay here?"

"Don't worry. I'll take care of them." Anastasia said, coming out with buckets of paint. "It's a new world, right? The people will have to reconsider what they think is possible."

"And we're nothing, compared to what is really possible, right?" Jaccapo said, coming out with a ladder. "Just you wait until they see a bear riding a magic-carpet snowboard!"

"Right," Maya agreed.

"We're going to put on a little show," said Anastasia. "A standing act. Or maybe traveling, if we have some success. —Saving Pine Tree Tjikko: The Demise of the Dark Boards."

"That's wonderful." Maya said. "Again, thank you everyone."

"For what?" Jaccapo said. "It was nothing."

"For being our friends," Maya said. "And for saving our lives multiple times. We owe you. So, if you ever are in need of help…"

"Yeah! You know how to contact us!" Adam said, speaking through the trumpet picture on his board.

The sound transmitted through the board of Anastasia. She lit up in a smile.

"Yeah the boards are 'capable of more than we know'," Adam said, holding up air quotes. "Freakin' ancient beings!" he mused.

"And if you ever want to see America," Maya said. "You're more than welcome. Bring your show. Spread the word!"

"I'll call you, Anastasia!" Adam said, excited.

"You better," Anastasia said, with a salty look.

Suddenly she pulled him close and kissed him with her soft wooden lips. When they ceased, they saw that everyone was looking at them weird.

"Is there something wrong?" Anastasia asked defiantly.

"It's just—" Tzara let out a long sigh. "It looks like we have some getting used to this, ourselves."

"Well said, Tzara," Maya said putting an arm on Tzara's shoulder.

Don't you start flirting with me, Maya!" He recoiled.

Maya laughed.

"Bye guys!" She said, with tears in her eyes, and bittersweet sound in her voice.

"Bye for now," the puppets said.

They walked away, turning back from time to time, to see the puppets painting in the pale afternoon sun. Some cars passed by and honked at each other. The pedestrians and the citizens went about their regular day. And soon the puppets passed out of sight, among the motion of the town.

Maya and Adam floated once again down that old country road in golden sun. They reconvened with Dharma, Ubuntu, Zeddefungo, and the people of the Tree of Life, who were relaxing in the shady grove.

"That was harder than I thought," Adam said.

"Come," Ubuntu said. "Don't feel the unconnection. They are—"

"—In my heart. I know," Adam said.

Ubuntu looked at Adam with his head down.

"Do you know what else?" Dharma added. "They never end. You will never really say goodbye. You'll see."

Adam lifted up his head, but his stare was still of many miles.

"Our poor state here," Ubuntu said to Dharma. Dharma agreed with poor compassion. "Forced to endure the sweet aching of time. I still don't know why."

"For the stories. For the memories." Zeddefungo stepped up, putting his arm on Adam's shoulder. "Beyond that I know not why. But the absence of this manifestation of chaos, into duality, from dark to light, and black and white to color... I know now is something worth enduring. When you found me in that trench... I was... —I was somewhere far worse than death," he said.

"Hell?" said Maya.

"I would have taken fire over this...abyss," Zeddefungo said. "Come," he said, in one more cheerful tone. "The mystery unfolds! The wonder is in the undeniability of its unknowableness! Until it unfolds, we follow..."

"The light?" Maya said.

"The light," Zeddefungo confirmed.

"I've missed you Zeddefungo!" Dharma said as she and Ubuntu laid their heads upon their brother's shoulder.

Maya put her arm around her own brother, and they rode off through the field together, followed by the joyous flock of warriors.

"To the Tree of Life!" Adam said.

Chapter 59

In the silver late morning sun the riders climbed from the jungle into the grass and crops of the great broad hill. Soon the Great Tree came into view, shining. Ubuntu took in a deep breath. Maya looked at Adam. They shared a feeling of homecoming, a feeling of wonder. Soon they could hear the soft sounds of voices, and the daily motion of the inhabitants, as they climbed higher, until the full vast glory of the tree was in their midst.

The children in the field looked once, and knew it was so. They had been waiting, hoping, every second for this day to come. They left their dolls and soccer balls, and sprinted to Ubuntu and her following of riders.

Children reunited with their parents who welcome them with open arms. Some women, some men, some elders left behind, lay down their work and join the riders in the field.

"It's good to be home," Ubuntu said to Dharma.

Nicu and Jatta meet their mother in the field with tears of joy, tears of loss.

"Kazzo..." Jatta's mother said, she looked. She knew, by the faces of her sons, that her husband was not to come home.

"His life was given for us, mama," Nicu said to her.

"He fought with so much courage," Jatta said. "I—," he started, but broke into tears.

His mother hugged him close, brought Nicu into the hug.

"He would have had it no other way," said their mother strongly. "He was born for it to end this way."

Jatta nodded.

"I will do my best to carry on his way," swore Jatta. "To care for you and Nicu. To never let us despair, as Father never would."

Mother hugged them both again.

"You will do a marvelous job."

Maya wandered near, greeting friends and meeting friends from the Tree.

"Maya!" Jatta called. "Remember Maya, Ma? The fútbol girl!"

"Maya," Jatta's mother said, and hugged her. She reached and smacked Jatta on the head. "Fútbol girl," she scolded.

Jatta winced, and wondered what he did wrong.

"She is responsible for our safe return, for our victory!" he said. Maya smiled and Jatta put his arm around her. "She is— amazing."

Jatta's mother smiled a warm smile towards Maya.

"She is no human, like they say," Jatta's mother said. "She is an angel." As she held her face and hugged her once again.

"Hey, I helped— Aaah forget it. Maya is amazing," Adam said, emerging from the crowd.

Ubuntu came behind him. Dharma followed, greeting many old friends.

"Isela, I am sorry for your loss," Ubuntu said to Jatta's mother. "May he receive good rest until you meet again. He sure does deserve it."

"Don't I know it," Isela said. She turned in wonder to see Dharma standing there. "Dharma?!" She rushed to her and gave her a loving hug.

"Isela. Your boys. They are— men," Dharma said. "It has been— has it been that long?"

"So long, Dharma," Isela smiled. "Long lost Dharma— what a day! We have so much to catch up on!"

"We found her hiding in the mountains again," Ubuntu said.

"Ooo Dharma, it's so cold up there!" Isela said.

"You're right about that!" Dharma said. "I'm thinking I might need to warm up for a while."

"You sure do!" Isela said. "You look white as snow. I just so happen to have an extra cot— now. God rest his soul. You really wanna stay?"

"I really wanna stay." Dharma said.

"Oh my— Dharma and Ubuntu in the Tree of Life, it's about to be lit," Isela said.

"The tree is already illuminated, Isela," Ubuntu smiled. "But yes, it will be wonderful."

"I'm not talking about those little lanterns, Ubuntu," Isela said. "—Hey Zeddefungo! You staying too?"

"I have to get back to my forest," Zeddefungo said. "I—"

"Shut up Zeddefungo, I heard you put all those demons to sleep!" Isela said.

"Well, I suppose, it's just a short tree trunk jump away," Zeddefungo said.

"Wooo, it's about to be the Tree of Life and Death and Heaven and Acapulco and Everything in between!" Isela said.

"This is my mother," Jatta said to Maya, as he shook his head.

"Boy, go clean the house— I don't think *you* saved the universe!" Isela said.

The party of riders made their way up into the tree, and filled the gathering places. Home at last, and it was as if nothing had changed. No time had gone by. But it was time for a lively celebration. The elders and the women brought out fruit and vegetables to the tables, and some cricket soup. Still a healthy alternative to the feasts of Tjikko Country. The riders shared their stories, as they swayed in arms of loved ones, held their children tight, dreamt of many days to come with smooth sailings, tranquil seas.

A peace would be ensured that had not been known in Jatta's, or even older of the men's long lives. There was peace before. Peace here and peace there, but always something that was known was temporary. A peace with reservations, always in the back of everyone's minds. A tightness they all knew, that deep down they had to hold, in preparation for each coming breaking of the peace. But this was different. They could feel it in the air. They could sense it from experience that this was a peace that they'd be sinking into, for some time to come.

Evening came and they still were hanging out. The sun was setting big red on the horizon, with purple stripes across its face. Dharma strolled along alone under the light of the amber lanterns. The insects of the jungle rang and chirped. She listened to the language of its texture, remembered that she used to know.

She walked until the waterfall and let her hand be covered in the mist. She sat beside the water until the moon rose high, and lively celebrators quieted, the wayward howl now and then of Isela reviving the simmering flame

"We should get that girl a board," Ubuntu said, walking up to Dharma. "We could have used her spirit out there!" She sat down next to Dharma looking at the stars.

"The world is changing now," Dharma said.

"Yes. And what is Dharma doing?" Ubuntu asked.

She thought a minute.

"I don't know," Dharma said, not knowing.

"Isn't that nice?" Ubuntu said.

They sat there for another while. Just listening to silence, warm silence of life. After a while, they walked back to the party, hand and hand until they came a little closer.

"I don't think we've held each other's hands since we were— kids," Ubuntu said.

"Just little girls," Dharma said, longingly. "We didn't have a care in the world."

They climbed the steps and joined the lovely company. Dharma watched as Maya and the kids all laughed and laughed. Maya noticed Dharma was back, and wandered over, stopping, hugging friends on the way.

"Mom, I love it here. And I want to visit all the time." Maya said, looking. "But.. I miss my home."

"I know, baby," Dharma answered. "You can visit any time, but its fine if you—"

"But—"Maya interrupted, "I was wondering... if... well, dad..." she paused, "we should... he would die to see you Mom. You have to— can you please come with us? I miss *home*-home." she said, tears filling her eyes.

The tears filled Dharma's eyes in turn.

"He..." Maya started.

"I don't know if I can," Dharma stared with compassion, confusion, hope, sorrow, joy, fear, pain and love all in one.

A tear fell down Maya's cheek. She looked at Dharma with all those feelings the same, but with something more beseeching, something beyond words, petitions only mother-daughters know.

"Alright." Dharma said, softly while a tear falls down her cheek. She hugged Maya. "I'll take you home," she said. "We can go tomorrow."

"I love you, mom." Maya said, as she closed her eyes and hugged her mother tightly.

Chapter 60

Maya woke up early. She looked at Adam lying in the other bed. In the low light of the morning she got out of bed. As she descended from the loft, she ran her hand along the banister. She went into each room one last time. She noticed details of the walls, and of the corners, of the rugs, and little imperfections in the furniture. Details she had no time to see before.

She walked out on the balcony, and sat down with the waking of the morning, the waking of the world, the birds, the wind. She looked out over as the lake was still but for a few quick ripples on its flatness, and barely light of grey over dark blue waters.

"Are you sure you wanna leave?" said Adam as soft as her awareness, coming out onto the deck.

Maya just smiled. Adam joined her in the other chair leaning back looking out. Two cranes made their way across the lake hanging low above calm waters.

"We could stay here for the summer, yeah?" Adam said, cracking a big smile at Maya.

"Yeah," Maya said, with a smile on her face.

Maya made their beds and said goodbye to the tree house one last time. Adam ate a bowl of fruit for breakfast at the coffee table. Nicu and Jatta arrived at the doorway.

"Knock, knock," Jatta said.

"Jatta!" Maya said.

"No, no don't get sentimental yet," Jatta said. "Nicu and I wanted to see if we could take you to our favorite place before you leave — if you have some time."

"Of course. We have time, yes!" Maya said, excited.

"Okay, come on," Jatta said.

The sun had popped up now, and shined its pale light in streams through the invisible mist of the morning, a pure white light. The world was still and picturesque, like a sketch by an impressionist painter. Jatta, Nicu, Maya and Adam, in noir animation, follow along a wide grassy path between trees as it bends and wanders, rises and falls through the woods.

"Our mother and father used to take us here when we were— babies," Jatta said.

And suddenly the path had opened up. It opened up to the top of a wide, wide hill. The hill was full of yellow grass, among a broad clearing in the trees, which opened to an even broader land of grass as far as the eye could see. The long grass waves in gentle wind. The sun shimmered as it fluttered.

Maya and Adam stood there, breathtaken at the rim of the hill.

"Wow." Maya said, in a sounding whisper.

The four stood still with boards in hands.

"Thank you, Maya, Adam." Jatta said to them. He stood still for a moment. "I come here once a week. Same day. Same time. For me this place is my metric. I know my universe, by how I know this place, when I come." Jatta looked at Maya and at Adam and said, "You have brought this back to life. I am seeing it now as I saw it all those years ago. Happy... Free... Thank you."

Maya looked out at the landscape.

"Now," Jatta said, in a very upbeat tone. "Would you like us to show you a real use of the board? This was practiced by the ancients. A very advanced tactic."

Jatta sat down on his board at the top of the hill. Maya and Adam looked at each other confused. Nicu sat down on his board. Jatta had a furrowed brow, but then broke into a beaming smile.

"It is called— fun!" Jatta yelled, "Loosen you up a little! Let us show you the *real* way of the Tree of Life!"

And with that Nicu grabbed the back of Jatta's board, as he pushed himself up over the rim and sliding down the face on long dry grass, hollering as he went. Maya and Adam wasted no time sprinting after and slipping their boards beneath their butts, and sliding down the hill behind them.

The four children slid and yipped and hooted in the golden sun, on golden hills. They returned to find Ubuntu standing underneath the grand Tree with Dharma and Zeddefungo.

"There you guys are," Dharma said.

"Jatta was showing us... the world before confusion," Maya said.

"The grass hill," Jatta said to Ubuntu.

"Just beautiful it is," Ubuntu said. She looked to Maya and Adam, standing there in all their splendor "Please, come back soon. We have so much more to show you."

"We will," Maya said. She gave Ubuntu a big long hug. "Thank you, Ubuntu, for everything!"

"Thank *you*, Maya, Adam," Ubuntu said. "What a beautiful heart you both share. And you can call me Aunt Ubuntu now, if you want," she smiled. "Please come back soon to check on this mother of yours, and me too!"

"We will," Adam and Maya said at the same time.

"I'll look after 'em while you're gone," Zeddefungo said. "I know how these two can get when their together."

"You mean they're not always so regal and wise?" Adam asked.

"They get loopy," Zeddefungo said.

"We'll be back for that for sure," Maya said. "See you later Ubuntu," Maya said, and gave another hug.

"See you soon sister," Dharma said. "Don't get too loopy without me."

Maya, Adam and Dharma hovered up the waterfall and made their way out of the jungle, into the grasslands, and over to the Baobab-Hyperion Connection.

"I hate this part," Zeddefungo said.

"I love this part," Dharma, jumping through the portal.

They warped themselves through space and time, or maybe just through the roots, or the minds of the plants.

Then they made their way through giant red sequoias, as they rode in the light of the high noon sun. They came to Zeddefungo's cave. Zeddefungo cruised onto the landing pad cliff with the comfortable air of homecoming.

"Alright, sis," Zeddefungo said. "Pick me up on your way back through. And good luck reuniting with your human husband, who you haven't seen in 15 years and thinks you're dead."

"Graceful," Dharma said.

"Thinks you're dead but actually a supernatural, flying board-riding warrior," Zeddefungo added.

"Yes, thank you. I will see you when I see you, Z," Dharma said.

Zeddefungo tipped his imaginary cap to her.

"Goodbye Zeddefungo, I'll never forget you," Adam said.

"Never forget you? I'll see you in like a week!" Zeddefungo said. "If you don't come to visit me, I'll come to you, you little... crazy— oh my little buddy. Oh, I love you, oh I'll miss you so much!" he said and then fell on Adam and hugged him. "I'll just come and visit you in a couple of days. Aaaah! Adam is my best friend! Dharma let his uncle take him. Please!"

"No chance," Dharma said.

"Good bye Zeddefungo," Maya said.

To which Zeddefungo straightened out a little.

"Good bye, good Maya," Zeddefungo continued, "—Best Maya. Best human, best rider, you're the greatest. I love you, too."

"Love you, Zeddefungo," Maya said as she laughed and gave him a hug.

Zeddefungo broke from Maya's hug with an awkward high five hand shake.

"See you brother," Dharma said and hugged him for good measure. "You know I love you."

"Oh yeah, we go way back," Zeddefungo laughed. "See yah later. I'll just be here cleanin' up ma' cave. Or maybe, I should mess it up a little," Zeddefungo said a little to himself. "Or maybe, I should check in on my main mountain lion," he said, even a little more now to himself.

Dharma, Maya and Adam took to the skies on their boards. The three of them together soaring high above the poofy clouds. Adam looked at Maya and they smiled. Maya looked at Dharma and they smiled. Dharma looked at Adam and they smiled. Free, they were all free. Just each other, their boards and the sun. Riding off into the distance.

Chapter 61

Dharma walks up the middle of a gray paved street, in a quiet neighborhood, with Adam close and Maya closer. It's evening in early summer. The sun was gold and coming down, casting an all-pervading tangerine glow. Down the hill, before them in the distance, all the trees and buildings have a screen of concrete-realistic filter to them in this light. And the black shadows of all objects are as bold as the light they balance against.

Kids ride by on bikes. Families walking dogs and strollers. Kids in front yards playing. Sprinklers shooting, water falling, making rainbows in the mist. It was quiet up here. No distant sound of highways, no one driving much. Just the people, just the laughter and the water and the breeze.

Dharma walks with flowing garments, light and pure. Her hair just flips a little as she walks but may as well be floating.

Then Maya points to him, her dad. She turns to Dharma, says something inaudible. He's outside, mowing the front lawn. Dharma's eyes are fixed on him with unspeakable, unthinkable love. The way the eye brows so slightly fold in and pull up in the middle.

He looks once, mowing, looks again and stops. He lets the lawn mower go, and stands. He knew the animation of his children's movements from a long way away. He was frozen in the grass. He knew it looked like something, but that wasn't... but what else could it be? He knew her movements too. He just has to break the reef of hope he holds himself below, for all these years, to maybe just be disappointed for the millionth time. He walked a little closer toward them. He didn't even let his psyche dream of this. He got a little closer. She... his reality begins to shatter in his periphery, all the rules are changing. He starts to run a little. The lifting of the veil is called *apocalypse*[3]. Dharma starts to run a little too. Maya looks at Adam, crying smiling galloping sprinting everybody, comes together in the middle of the street. They met, they hugged— and kissed. They held each other tight. There were no words, only music, the language of spirits. The world was spinning around her in his arms. The kids now join the love, as dad brings everybody in.

"I don't understand," he says. "But I don't care. It doesn't even matter. I mean, you can tell me, but it doesn't even matter." He held her face and her arms, to feel that she was real. "Sophia... you... you're here!"

He held her tight.

"I'm here," she said, hugging back, squeezing her eyes closed tight and smiling.

"Adam, Maya," he smiled "—What is happening?" he asked them. "Am I dead? Wait am I— are we dead?"

"I don't know," Dharma said.

He hugged her once again and laughed 'til tears of joy came out.

"Come on, let's go inside," he said.

A family once again, they walk from out of the street into the front yard, already fast at play, Dad with Adam chasing, Mom with her arm around Maya. They're there.

In the kitchen Maya stands. She feels like she is three again. She feels like she is in the vision she was having on the battle field. The white silk curtain stream and flutter in the breeze. The white kitchen shines with evening sun through curtain silk. She pours them lemonade. She looks out in the yard at four chairs always empty, filled today.

Adam and Dad are putting firewood in the pit and starting a fire. Mom is near, slowly walking through the yard, looking at the trees, and then the boys, and then inside to Maya. Adam throws a football her way, which she catches, laughs and throws back at him hard. Maya grabs the tray of lemonade and s'mores. She closes her eyes. She steps through the doorway, and into the backyard.

Chapter 62

In a corner office, on the 50th floor of a mirrored glass sky scraper downtown, pale hands with blue veins are typing on a computer. Periodically shuffling papers on the desk beside him. Outside, the sun has set. Darkness falls. He inspects a piece of paper, lays it down, and scratches his signature of approval on the document.

A man in a navy suit, light blue shirt, red tie, leans through the doorway into the corner office, leather bag around his shoulder.

"Don't stay too late Mark, its Friday you know," the man says.

The man at the desk looks momentarily. His hands still poised at paper.

"They install a dimmer in your office? I gotta talk to somebody about that." The man in the doorway continues. "Alright, see yah Monday."

He leaves the doorway, walks down the aisle of cubicles outside. The cleaning crew have already begun to vacuum.

The pale white hands now close the laptop carefully, collect the papers, knock them on the desk to straighten the stack, and place them in a black tight briefcase.

Another man appears at the door, seeming to float into position so silently and swift.

"Excuse me sir," the man says. "Your presence is requested at his estate. Tomorrow evening. Nine o' clock."

"Understood," says pale hands.

The man in the doorway floats away.

Shiny black shoes now walk down the thin film of commercial carpet over concrete, under fluorescent LED lightbulbs.

Soon they make their way out through giant glass front doors and on to city sidewalks broad, surrounded by the sound of engines, horns and rushing people, the glow of advertisements bright.

He steps into the back of one black window tinted BMW.

"Where to, sir?" says a granular voice from the driver's seat, turning facing back.

"Home, of course," says the man in the back seat. "And wipe your mouth you filthy animal, you're getting drool on everything."

Chapter 63

"Maya?" Mr. Rainer calls. He walks up wooden steps. "Mayaa?" Mr. Rainer calls again.

"Be right out!" Maya calls from muffled bathroom.

Mr. Rainer smiles looking at the family photos now in upstairs hallway. He floats in bliss this evening. He turns to see that Maya's door is open and he wanders mindlessly over there. Again, with no good reason he just looks inside, and turns to go back to the campfire. But he sees something. Maya's driftwood board is leaning in the corner under clothes.

He holds the board turning it over in his hands, admiring this updated design. He puts the board down on the ground for fun and fakes riding down a hill. He can't ride it though. The board won't work for humans. Then all the sudden, a purple glow appears. He stares in impressed confusion. Suddenly he's in the air. He crashes off the wall and knocks things off the dresser.

"Mayaaa!" Mr. Rainer shouts.

Maya, washing hands, looks up into the mirror.

www.ingramcontent.com/pod-product-compliance
Lightning Source LLC
Chambersburg PA
CBHW071618150726
48000CB00004B/1780